KARPURAMANJARI

KARPURAMANJARI

(THE PRAKRIT PLAY OF RAJASEKHARA)

Critically edited with an Introduction and Notes

By

MANOMOHAN GHOSH, M. A., Ph. D.

Lecturer, Calcutta University

GYAN

Published by

GYAN

Gyan Publishing House
5, Ansari Road
Daryaganj, New Delhi-110002
Phone: 011-47034999, 9811692060
E-mail: books@gyanbooks.com

Distribution Network
gyanbooks.com
India, USA, Canada, UK, Australia, France

ISBN : 978-81-212-6278-1 (PB)
First Published, 1939

2nd Impression 2022

Printed at: Gyan Press, Delhi.

KARPURAMANJARI
Author: MANOMOHAN GHOSH

KARPURAMANJARI

(THE PRAKRIT PLAY OF RAJASEKHARA)

Critically edited with an Introduction and Notes

by

MANOMOHAN GHOSH, M. A., Ph. D.

Lecturer, Calcutta University

1939

BY THE SAME EDITOR

1. **Abhinayadarpana** of Nandikeśvara, *a manual of gestures and postures used in ancient Indian dance and drama* (Calcutta Sanskrit Series, No. V.).

2. **Caturangadipika** of Śūlapāṇi, *a manual of four-handed dice-chess* (Calcutta Sanskrit Series, No. XXI.).

3. **Paniniya Siksa** or the Śikṣā-Vedāṅga ascribed to Pāṇini, *the most ancient work on Indo-Aryan Phonetics* (Calcutta University).

4. **Medieval Mysticism of India,** *translation of Prof. Kshitimohan Sen's* ভারতীয় মধ্যযুগে সাধনার ধারা (Luzac & Co.).

DEDICATED

TO

Prof. Dr. SUNITI KUMAR CHATTERJI

CONTENTS

ACKNOWLEDGMENTS

It is my most pleasant duty to record here thanks to those who in one way or other has given me help in the preparation of this volume. In this connexion I should mention first the name of Dr. Syamaprasad Mookerjee during whose Vice-Chancellorship the work was undertaken. He took great interest in the work and gave me the necessary facility for its completion. I am very genuinely grateful to him for his kindness. Next I should offer my sincere thanks to Mr. Jogeschandra Chakravorti, M. A., the Registrar of the Calcutta University. It is due to him that this volume has been very promptly published. I am also to give thanks to my pupil Mr. D. E. Hettiaratchi, B. A. (Lond.) for he has pointed out to me some misprints which escaped my notice. Last but not the least I should express my most respectful thanks to my teacher Prof. Dr. Suniti Kumar Chatterji for his occasional advice and suggestion during the preparation of this work. It is however needless to add that for all views expressed in it the responsibility is entirely mine.

The Editor

BIBLIOGRAPHY

Alsdrof, L. (ed.)—Kumārapālapratibodha, Hamburg. 1922.

Annals of the Bhandarkar Oriental Research Institute.

Apte, V. S.—A Guide to Sanskrit, Bombay, 1913.
Sanskrit-English Dictionary, Bombay, 1924.

Basak, R. G.—The History of North-Eastern India, Calcutta, 1934.

Bhagavad-gītā.

Bhāmaha—Kāvyālaṅkāra (Nirnayasagar ed.)

Bloch, Jules—La formation de la langue marathe, Paris, 1914.

Bulletin of the School of Oriental Studies.

Catalogue of Sanskrit Mss. in the India Office Library.

Carpentier, J. (ed.)—Uttarādhyayana-sūtra, Uppsala, 1922.

Chatterji, S. K.—Origin and Development of the Bengali Language, Calcutta, 1926.

Cowell, E. B. (ed.)—Prākṛtaprakāśa.

De, S. K.—Sanskrit Poetics, Vol. I, London, 1923.

Emeneau, M. B. (ed.)—Jambhaladatta's Version of the Vetālapañcaviṃśati. New Haven, 1934.

Gaṇgādharabhaṭṭa's commentary to the Gāthāsaptaśati—(Nirnayasagar ed.)

Garuḍa-purāṇa—(Vaṅgavāsī ed.)

Geiger, W.—Pāli Literatur und Sprache, Strassburg, 1916.

Ghosh, M. (ed.)—Abhinayadarpaṇa, Calcutta, 1934.

Ghosh, M.—Mahārāṣṭrī, a late phase of Śaurasenī, Calcutta, 1933.

Grierson, Sir G.—An Introduction to the Maithili Dialect of the Bihari Language as spoken in North Bihar, Part I, Calcutta, 1909.

Grierson, Sir G.—On the Modern Indo-Aryan Vernaculars, British India Press, Bombay, 1933.

Haas, G. C. O. (ed.)—Daśarūpa, New York, 1912.

Seth, Haragovinddas—Pāiasaddamahaṇṇavo, Calcutta, 1928.

Hemacandra—Kavyānuśāsana (Nirnayasagar ed.)

" Prākrit Grammar (ed. Pischel).

Hertel, J. (ed.)—Muṇḍaka Upaniṣad, Leipzig, 1924.

Hillebrandt, A. (ed.)—Mudrārākṣasa, Breslau, 1911. Neudruck, 1925.

Hoernle, R.—A Grammar of the Eastern Hindi compared with the other Gauḍian Languages, London, 1880.

" Prākṛtalakṣaṇa (Bibliotheca Indica).

Indian Antiquary.

Indian Historical Quarterly.

Jacobi, H. (ed.)—Ācārāṅga-sūtra, London, 1882.

" Bhavisattakaha, Munich, 1918.

" Kalpa-sūtra, Leipzig, 1879.

" Sanatkumāracarita, Munich, 1921.

Journal of the American Oriental Society.

Journal of the Department of Letters, Calcutta University.

Kālidāsa—Meghadūta, Ṛtusaṃhāra.

Keith, A. B.—Sanskrit Drama, Oxford, 1924.

Kellog, A.—Grammar of the Hindi Language (2nd edition) London, 1893.

Konow, Sten (ed.)—Karpūramañjarī (HOS), 1901.

Lüders, H,—Brückstücke der buddhistische Dramen, Berlin, 1910.

Mammaṭabhaṭṭa—Kāvyaprakāśa.

Mārkaṇḍeya—Prākṛtasarvasva (ed. Bhaṭṭanātha Svāmī), Vizagapatam, 1912.

Nāṭyaśāstra, ascribed to Bharata (Chowkhamba ed.)

Nobel, J.—Foundations of Indian Poetry, Calcutta, 1923.

Paṇdit (Old Series).

Patañjali,—Mahābhāṣya (ed. Kielhorn).

Pāṭhak Commemoration Volume.

Pischel, R.—Grammatik der Prākrit-sprachen.

Prākṛta-paiṅgala, (Bibliotheca Indica).

Printz—Bhāsa's Prākrit, Frankfurt A. M. 1921.

Rājaśekhara—Bālabhārata (Nirnayasagar ed.)

,, Bālarāmāyaṇa (ed. Jīvānanda).

,, Karpūramañjarī (,,)

,, ,, (Nirnayasagar ed.)

,, ,, (ed. Konow).

,, Kāvyamīmāṃsā (3rd. Baroda ed.)

,, Viddhaśālabhañjikā (ed. Jīvānanda).

Rudraṭa—Kāvyālaṅkāra (Nirnayasagar ed.)

Saṅgītaratnākára (Ānandāśrama ed.)

Shastri, H. P.—বৌদ্ধগান ও দোহা, Calcutta, 1923 B. E.

Swami, N.—Rājasthān-rā Dūhā, Delhi, 1935.

Todar Mall (ed.)—Mahāvīracarita, London, 1928.

Turner, R. L.—Position of Romani in Indo-Aryan, London, 1926.

V a r m a, Siddheshwar—Critical Studies in the Phonetic Observation of Indian Grammarians, London, 1929.

V ā t s y ā y a n a—Kāmasūtra (Vaṅgavāsī ed.)

W a c k e r n a g e l, J.—Altindische Grammatik. Vol. I. Goetingen 1896.

W e b e r, A.—Ueber ein Fragment der Bhagavatī. Berlin, 1865.

W h i t n e y, W. D.—Sanskrit Grammar, London, 1896.

W i n t e r n i t z, M.—History of Indian Literature, Vol. I, Calcutta, 1926.

ABBREVIATIONS

Ap. =Apabhraṃśa.
Beng. =Bengali.
Bālar. =Bālarāmāyaṇa.
IHQ =Indian Historical Quarterly.
JAOS =Journal of the American Oriental Society,
JDL =Journal of the Department of Letters, Calcutta University.
K. =KM. as reconstructed by Sten Konow.
Kāvyamī. =Kāvyamīmāṃsā of Rājaśekhara.
KM. =Karpūramañjarī.
Lanman =Lanman's Translation of the Karpūra-mañjarī.
M. =Mahārāṣṭrī Pkt.
Mahārāṣṭrī =Mahārāṣṭrī, a late phase of Śaurasenī by Manomohan Ghosh in JDL.
MIA. =Middle Indo-Aryan.
NIA. =New Indo-Aryan.
Pkt. =Middle Indo-Aryan of the Second Period.
Rāj. =Rājaśekhara.
Ś. =Śaurasenī.
Viddh. =Viddhaśālabhañjikā.
Vr. =Vararuci's Prākṛtaprakāśa.

N. B. *References to the KM. in the Introduction and Notes usually relate to Prof. Konow's edition.*

INTRODUCTION

I. General

1. *The Present Edition.* In his preface to the Karpūramañjarī published in the Harvard Oriental Series Prof. Lanman writes:

"A critical edition of the Karpūramañjarī is an urgent necessity for the advancement of Prākrit studies." Thus wrote Pischel in 1879, in the preface to his Hemachandra p. xii. For the realization of his long-deferred hope, we have at last to thank one of his own pupils, Dr. Sten Konow, whose work, as I trust, will clearly show the training in rigorous philological method which he has received at the hands of his eminent master (p. xiv).

Hence any attempt to edit the KM. afresh, strongly calls for an explanation. It is true that the work was edited by a very competent scholar and from a good number of mss. of different recensions, but more than thirty-five years being past since Prof. Konow's critical edition of the KM. was published (1901), and discovery of new data during the time as well as researches by various investigators having considerably modified some of the findings of earlier scholars on which Konow, Pischel and others had to depend, a new edition of the KM. in the light of later researches will parhaps not be considered unnecessary. For example, it is no longer possible after the discovery of the Buddhist drama-fragments by Lueders and the fragments of the Pkt. Dhammapada by Dutreuil de Rhins, to maintain an orthodox attitude about the exhaustiveness of the ancient Pkt. grammars (see Pischel, Grammatik, pp. 45-49). For it is evident that, serviceable though they have been in their own way much have escaped the notice of authors of such works. Yet it was according to the dictum of these grammars rather than after the oldest and best ms. that modern editors[1] (of Pkt. works) including Konow have up till now tried to correct their texts. Thus we find that in numerous passages Konow rejected the testimony of his best ms. on the plea that it went against grammatical rules. It will be shown later on (§ 11) that since Pkt. grammarians have not taken into notice all the various kinds of Pkt. current or available in literature in their time and since they have confined themselves only to a few late dialetcts neglecting others, their rules should not have the same binding force on our texts (unlike what we are entitled to do in the case of classical Sanskrit, where insistence on the rules of grammar can be legitimately made) and hence they should be used very cautiously in rectifying the alleged errors of mss. (cf. Konow, pp. 202-203).

2. But this procedure by itself cannot be said to have injured much Konow's edition of the KM. The saddest harm came from elsewhere.[2] The antiquity of the tradi-

---

1. There are, however, some notable exceptions. J. Charpentier in his critical edition of the Uttarādhyayanasūtra, Uppsala, 1922, seems to have followed the best ms. Johannes Hertel has very strongly protested against the procedure of correcting Prakrit texts according to Prakrit grammars. ('Muṇḍaka Upaniṣad', Indo-Iranische Quellen und Forschungen, Heft III. Leipzig, 1924, pp. 7-8).

2. Another aspect of Konow's edition that should be mentioned here is his well-intentioned introduction of the peculiar forms of the two dialects (Mahārāṣṭrī and Śaurasenī) even against the reading of all mss. (p. xxii).

tion about the use of Mahārāṣṭrī in metrical Pkt. portions of a drama has been accepted by most scholars without any question. In following this tradition Sten Konow was badly misled in his reconstruction of the text of the KM. For in opposition to the testimony of the mss., including the best one, he made violent changes in the orthography of the metrical portions of the play to give it a Mahārāṣṭrī feature. Though such an interference with the testimony of mss. is against the accepted principles of textual criticism[1], yet for reasons stated above Konow felt justified about it. It will be shown below (§ 21) that the dictum about the use of M. in the metrical Pkt. passages of a drama, which later became a tradition (at least in later works on poetics), is not earlier than the tenth century and probably much later, and hence Rājaśekhara had no chance of following it. Besides this we learn that a saṭṭaka should be written in *one* language which should be neither M. nor Skt.[2] Thus we find that the KM. was written entirely in Ś.

3. The mss. of Pkt. works though they appear often to be full of mistakes are, in many cases, not really so

---

1. See note 1 in p. 2. Hertel's view in a way strengthens the accepted principles of textual criticism in case of Pkt. works.

2. In his Kāvyānuśāsana H e m a c a n d r a defines the saṭṭaka as follows :

viṣkambhakapraveśaka-rahito vastv ekabhāṣayā bhavati /
a-prākṛta-saṃskṛtayā sa saṭṭako nāṭikā-pratimaḥ //

(p. 325, ed. Kāvyamālā)

The word 'Prākṛta' in this quotation means M. For in his grammar Hemacandra does not use the term Mahārāṣṭrī and treats this under the name 'Prākṛta' (see, śeṣaṃ p r ā k ṛ t a - vat, iv, 286).

and in spite of their several apparently questionable aspects (which are not many) they are ordinarily good guides in reconstructing a text. The real significance of the corrupt nature of Pkt. mss. will be explained later on (§§ 12-19). It was probably due to the apparently confusing nature of the mss. of the KM. that Konow did not venture to take any ms. as the basis of his critical edition, and he reconstructed the text in, what may be called, an eclectic fashion. But such a procedure in the critical reconstruction of texts is not commendable. And the best ms. of the KM. as we shall see later on (§ 8) represents the author more faithfully than Konow or Pischel could ever have imagined.

These, then, are the principal points on which a fresh critical edition of the KM. may be justified. Besides these there are others too. In spite of the great care and caution bestowed on the work by Profs. Lanman and Konow a few passages have still remained without any satisfactory explanation. An attempt has therefore been made here to throw fresh light on them. The literary merit and the personality of Rāj. has also been judged from a new stand-point, and fresh materials like the Kāvyamīmāṃsā have been used for the purpose.

4. It should, however, be mentioned here that, though in the Harvard edition of the KM. there has now been discovered scope for some improvement, it has the honour of serving most gloriously the cause of Pkt. studies for the last thirty-five years, and the present editor is fully conscious of his deep debt to the work which considerably stimulated his enquiry in the domain of Pkt. philology, and begs apology of Profs. Sten Konow and C. R. Lanman for his occasional criticism of their views. Our constant reference to their joint work will most

clearly demonstrate how indispensable it will remain for some time to come for the study of this important text.

5. *The Critical Apparatus.* As our principle of reconstructing the text of the KM. has been different from that adopted by Konow, we could use, in addition to some new materials, all that he very carefully collated for a critical study of the work. The following is a short account of the eleven mss. of the text which he used. This is based on his Critical Account of the Manuscripts, (pp. xxiii-xxvi).

A. Devanāgarī ms. See Bhandarkar, Report on the search for Skt. mss. in the Bombay Presidency during 1882-1883, Bombay 1884, p. 156, no. 418. An incorrect ms. Aspirates are doubled ; *nd* is often substituted for *nt*. This ms. comes from a Jain source.

B. Devanāgarī ms. Pkt. text, Skt. translation, and some glosses. Contains Act I. the beginning of II. as far as h i d a ā v a j j a ṃ (II, 1) and the end from s ā r a y a ṇ a m a y ī (IV. 19). See Kielhorn, Report on the search for Skt. mss. in the Bombay Presidency during 1880-81, Bombay, 1881, p. 83, no. 22. Date Saṃ. 1600. The ms. comes from a Jain source. According to Konow this is very corrupt. But in spite of this fact the ms. B often gives valuable help in reconstructing the text, especially in some few places where our best ms. fails to satisfy us.

C. Devanāgarī ms. See Bhandarkar, l.c. p. 156, no. 419. Contains Act II, This ms. has the same peculiarities as A and seems to be its continuation. The ms. comes from a Jain source.

N. A modern Devanāgarī ms. Text with a Skt. translation. Conclusion of the text is wanting. See Weber,

Verzeichniss der Sanskrit- und Prakrit-handschriften der Koeniglichen Bibliothek in Berlin, Berlin, 1886, no. 1558. The aspirates and occasional writing of *nd* for *nt* point to a South Indian origin; and forms such as d i ṃ n n a for d i ṃ b h a and a few instances of ya-śruti show influence from Jain mss.

O. A modern Devanāgarī ms. Prakrit text with some glosses. Sometimes corrections in the margin. In a few places defective. See Aufrecht, Catalogue of the Bodleian mss. p, 146b, no. 313.

P. Copy from a Jain ms. Complete text and translation. Modern and very incorrect. See Kielhorn, l.c. p. 83, no. 23.

R. Copy of the ms. No. 417 of the Raghunātha temple library. See Stein, Catalogue of the Sanskrit Manuscripts in the Raghunātha temple library of his Highness the Maharaja of Jammu and Kashmir, Bombay, 1894, p. 77, incorrect; some lacunas; conclusion wanting. Text with the commentary of Vāsudeva.

W. Devanāgarī ms. from a Jain source. Complete text with marginal paraphrase. See, Weber no. 1557. Date, Saṃvat 1528[1] varṣe śāke. The groups *ṭṭh* and *ddh* are as a rule not to be distinguished in this ms. Prof Konow has not properly appreciated the value of this ms. and has omitted to mention its other features. It uses *dy* for *jj* and often writes short *e* and short *o* as *i* and *u* respectively. Its occasional use of single consonants for double ones should be noticed. This is the oldest (*c.* 1470 A. C.) among the mss. of the KM. available at present and is the best one. We have discussed below (§ 8) its value.

---

1. Prof. Konow dates it wrongly as Saṃ. 1520.

S. Copy of the Tanjore ms. no. 10634. Grantha text with some lacunas. See Burnell, Classified index to the Skt. mss. in the palace at Tanjore, London, 1880, p. 168[a].

T. Copy of the Tanjore ms. no. 5253. Complete text. Some lacunas. Very incorrect. See Burnell, l.c.

U. Copy of the Tanjore ms. 10633[a], Grantha text with Skt. version. Some lacunas. See Burnell, l.c.

Of these eleven mss. we have made a first-hand study of the oldest mss. W (from a rotographic copy) and O (in original). For the readings of the other nine mss. we depended on copious notes which Konow gives from his excellent collation at the foot of the text of his edition.

In addition to materials handled by Konow we have used eight new mss. of which four are in Devanāgarī and four in Southern scripts, Grantha, Malayalam and Telugu. Of the Devanāgarī mss. three belong to the Northern recension, and the remaining one as well as mss. written in Southern scripts belong to the Southern recension. These mss. are being described below.

D. Devanāgarī ms. in the possession of the Royal Asiatic Society of Bengal. A modern ms. (written in Saṃvat 1887), 9.8″ × 6.5″. Countrymade paper, bound like a modern book in full leather. The volume contains other works besides the KM. It bears the no. I-E. 25 in the Society's own collection. This volume was formerly in the possession of the now defunct Fort William College of Bengal, for it bears a stamp in Urdu (Kt'b K'lj Fwrṭ Wlym), in Devanāgarī (Kitāb Kālij Forṭ Valiyam), and in Bengali characters (Pustak Kālej Phorṭ Uilyam).

This ms. gives a chāyā up to tā iha uvavisadu vaassa, (ed. Konow, II. 29[16]). It is not very carefully written but has an unmistakable resemblance to the ms. O of Konow and does not add to our knowledge of the text. Its conclusion is as follows :

V i d ū. bho vaassa bhāmario dijjantu huavahe lājahomo kiradu.

R ā j ā. (yathoktaṃ[1] nāṭayati).

B h a i r a. (Rājānaṃ prati) kiṃ te bhūyaḥ priyam upakaromi (?).

R ā j ā. bhaavaṃ tuha pasāeṇa esā laddhā.

R ā j ñ ī. pariṇedu maharāo savvāṇaṃ paccakkho.

R ā j ā. (Karpūramaṃjarīṃ pariṇīya yoginaṃ prati saṃskṛtam āśritya) svāmiṃs tvacaaraṇāravinda-vaśataḥ śṛṅgārasaṃjīvinī laddhā paṃcaśarapriyā nanu mayā Karpūramañjary asau / tallābhena ca cakravarti-padavī loke samāsāditā kiṃ kiṃ neha karoti...... mahatāṃ sandarśanaṃ jantuṣu //

iti niḥkrāntā sarve caturthaṃ yavanikāntaraṃ. samāptā ceyaṃ Karpūramañjarī, saṃvat 1878.

G. Devanāgarī ms. in the Library of the India Office, London. See India Office Catalogue no. 4163.

This ms. resembles most the ms. N of Konow. We are giving below its conclusion which is very similar to that of N.

V i d ū. bho vaassa bhāmario dijjaṃdu, hudabahe lājāṃjaliao chippaṃdu.

R ā j ā. (bhramaṇaṃ nāṭayati).

K a r p ū r a m a ñ j a r ī. (dhūmena vyāvṛtamukhī tiṣṭhati).

---

1. Punctuation, and brackets enclosing stage directions in this and the following extracts do not occur in mss.

V i d ū. dijjatū ācāli ācaliassa dakkhiṇā.

R ā j ā. vaassa gāma-sahassaṃ diṇṇaṃ.

V i d ū. sotthi hodo (iti nṛtyati).

B h a i r a. mahārāa uṇo vi ki te piaṃ kuṇemi.

R ā j ā. joīsara avaraṃ kiṃ piaṃ vaṭṭadi, kuṃtale × × karapphaṃsapphara-sokkha-siṭhilīkae-sagge(?) pālayami(?)-a mahīala-rajjaṃ cakkavaṭṭi-paaviramaṇijjaṃ, taha-vi edaṃ bhodu ;

sattho ṇaṃdaṃdu sajjaṇāṇa saalo vaggo khalāṇaṃ khijjadi, bahmaṇajaṇo sahummi-o(?) savvadā /

meho muṃcatu saṃciaṃ pi salilaṃ sassa(?)yiam bhūalaṃ loo loha loha-paraṃmuho'ṇudiahaṃ dhamme mahim(?) paadu // (iti niḥ-krāntāḥ sarve).

caturtha-javanikāntaraṃ. samāptam idaṃ Karpūra-maṃjarī-saṭṭakam.

The existence of the last passage (sattho ṇaṃdaṃdu etc.) uttered by the king in the ms. N has been attested by its chāyā (see Konow, p. 114). This ms. is not carefully written and has many lacunas. It does not add to our knowledge of the text of the KM.

I. Devanāgarī ms. in the library of the India Office, London. See India Office Catalogue no. 4162.

This ms. agrees to a great extent with the ms. R used by Konow. It often omits the anusvāra and substitutes *d* for *ṭṭ*. It seems however to have been contaminated by O, for the conclusion agrees to some extent with that of the latter (O), and is as fallows :

V i d ū. bho vaasaa vamirā dijjattu huavahe lājāhomo hoṇu.

R ā j ā. (tathaiva bhramaṇaṃ nāṭayati).

K—3

N ā y i k ā. (salajjam avanatamukhī).

(vivāhaṃ nirvartya sotsāhaṃ yathārham abhyarcya sarvān visarjya cakravartī bhūtvā tayoḥ saha rājyaṃ cakre).

B h a i r a. (rājānaṃ prati) kiṃ te bhūpaḥ priyam upakaromi.

R ā j ā. tuha pasāeṇa laddhā esā.

R ā j ñ ī. (sakalam avagatya) pariṇīdā(?)mahārāeṇa Kappūramaṃjarī tumhāṇam [pa]ccakkham asudvaram-ahappiam (?).

R ā j ā. (yoginaṃ prati saṃskṛtam āśritya)

svāmiṃś taccaraṇāravindavaśataḥ śṛṅgārasaṃjīvinī
labdhā paṃcaśarapriyā nanu mayā Karpūramaṃjaryasau /
tallābhena ca cakravarti-padavī loke samāsāditā
kiṃ kiṃ neha karoti mahatāṃ sandarśanaṃ prāniṣu //

This ms. too does not add to our knowledge of the text of the KM.

J. Devanāgarī ms. in the library of the India Office, London. It is a recent copy of some South Indian ms. and resembles the mss. T and U of Konow except in the verse at the conclusion. The concluding verse in this ms. is the same as that in the ms.S of Sten Konow. See India Office Catalogue no. 7378. This ms. too does not add to our knowledge of the text of the KM.

X. Telugu ms., palm-leaf pothi in the library of the India Office, London. See India Office Catalogue no. 7379. The conclusion of this ms. agrees with that of J described above, and TU of Konow. But in other matters it occasionally differs slightly from J. This ms. is not at all accurate, and has suffered gravely from worm-holes. This ms. does not know s t h ā p a k a which appears in TU of Sten Konow and in J. On this point alone the ms. gives a new information.

Y. Telugu ms., palm-leaf pothi in the library of the India Office, London. See India Office Cotalogue no. 7380. This ms. agrees very much with X but does not know any s t h ā p a k a. This is the only important feature of the ms.

Z. Malayalam ms., palm-leaf pothi in the library of the India Office, London. See India Office Catalogue no. 8197. The conclusion of this ms. is shorter than that of the rest of the mss. of the Southern recension. It lacks the verses 23 and 24 of the Act IV, (ed, Konow). It resembles partly T. and to a very small extent S. But unlike these mss. it has s ū t r a d h ā r a instead of sthāpaka. As sthāpaka is a familiar figure in mss. of plays available in Kerala, his total non-existence in this ms. hailing in all likelihood from the same place may be said to give us enough ground for presumption that the original work of Rāj. knew no sthāpaka who has been introduced into the work by some late interpolator. For details on this point see § 25. In this point alone the ms. has given valuable help in reconstructing the text.

V. Grantha ms., palm-leaf pothi in the library of the Visvabharati, Santiniketan. It bears the number 2210. The ms. is worm-eaten and very much worn out. With great difficulty we examined the beginning and the end. It resembles the ms. T of Konow very much and has s t h ā p a k a only after the second verse in the beginning. It does not seem to be a carefully written ms. It has a tendency to substitute words which are not to be found in any of the rest of the mss. (Northern or Southern) hitherto used. For example it has viaḍḍha for chaïlla (I. 1[b]) and ṇavaraṃ for kevalaṃ (I. 6[b]). It is sure that some interpolator tried his skill in Pkt. in this ms. or its prototype. This ms. too does not add to our knowledge of the text.

6. Besides the eight mss. not used by Konow we have examined afresh the three printed texts of the KM. published in India. Among them the *editio princeps* which appeared in the Pandit, Old Series, vol. vii (1872) is uncritical. It seems to have been prepared from a ms. agreeing more or less closely with N. of Konow. This printed text could scarcely be used for any improvement. The edition published from the Nirnayasagar Press (First edition in 1887 and the Second edition in 1900) resembles most the mss. NR of Konow. Though it cannot be called a critical edition it may be said to have retained its ms. value. The good edition of Vāsudeva's commentary which it prints has been of much help. The edition published by Jīvānanda Vidyāsāgar in 1889 is however of no value. The new commentary it gives is sometimes misleading.

But, as the ms. materials used in connection with the present edition are not of equal value we shall discuss below their relative merit. The fact that Konow has not given any clear and explicit conclusion or opinion about the relative authenticity of his mss. requires that we shall include them also in our discussion. For the sake of convenience let us take them first.

7. The chief characteristic of the Southern recension of the KM. mss., as has been pointed out by Konow, is the conclusion of the play. It is either altogether

missing or different in the mss. of the Northern recension (Konow, p. xxv). Any consideration of the relative value of the mss. of the KM. should be preceded by a discussion of the relative authenticity of the two available recensions. Following the familiar principle of the textual criticism that *the shorter text is, other things being equal, to be preferred to the longer*, we may at once assume that the mss. of the Northern recesion which lack the conclusion occurring in the Southern recension follow Rāj.'s original composition better than the other mss., and the mss. of the Southern recension having the longest conclusion are of less value than those of the Northern one. Konow too in spite of his adoption of the conclusion[1] or epilogue given in the Southern recension (as against its absence in the Northern one) in his edition has indirectly given his verdict against the same. For example in the prologue to the KM. Konow rejects the peculiar readings of the Southern recension in thirteen cases quoted below[2] :

I. 1^b pavaṭṭadu ; 3^b o ; 4^2 jaṇo dīsai ; 4^9 sajjiaṃdi ; 4^{10}°apphālopphālaṇa ; 4^{11}°gīdaaṃ ; 4^{16}dīsaha ; 6^a bhaṇijjai 7^a suumālo ; 7^b tattia ; 9^a ṇibbharadevassa ; 10^b vi dhavaledi ; 10^1 aṇuciṭṭhaha ;

---

1. The conclusion of the play or the Bharatavākya according to the testimony of the Nāṭyaśāstra is not necessarily an integral part of it. Hence its interpolation in the mss. of a play can easily be assumed. For details see Manomohan G h o s h , 'The Bharatavākya', IHQ, Vol. VI. 1930. pp. 485, 486.

2. References cited below and ever afterwards in the Introduction will be, unless otherwise mentioned, to the Harvard ed. of the KM.

As against this he accepts only rarely (e. g. in I. 15[b] °s ī m a n t i ṇ ī ṇ a ṃ) the testimony of the Southern recension. Though it is not possible to agree with Konow as regards his acceptance or rejection of particular readings we can consider his judgment about the value of the Southern recension as fundamentally correct. But even if this Southern recension is inferior to the Northern one, it is not without its value. For, in a very small number of cases, it supports the readings of our best ms. as against the inferior or later mss. of the Northern recension, and in some rare cases it seems to have retained the original reading better than its rival recension.

But the inferiority of the Southern mss. is not quite due to verbal interpolation only. Such interpolation and emendation indeed there are, but emendations occur not unoften in the matter of orthography too. Hence we find that in many cases these mss. substitute phonetically developed forms for older or archaic ones. A systematic occurrence of this phenomenon more or less in mss. of all the Pkt. works surely deserves our closest attention and should not at all be hastily ascribed to the carelessness or ignorance of scribes. We shall try later on (§ 8) to account for a systematic substitution of developed forms in a ms., and it may be assumed for the present that *later the ms. the more developed are its forms phonetically*. So much so that Ś. passages of a work in its very late mss. has often the chance of appearing as M. (See the various readings of verses 20, 21, 108, 134, 135 and 155 of the Mudrārākṣasa in the edition of A. Hillebrandt). Considered from this point of view also the Southern recension seems to be much younger in age than the Northern one. The following are a few cases where the Southern recension read phonetically developed forms :

I.	2^{a}	ḍaṃbarāi	for	ḍambarāiṃ[1]
	3^{a}	°ṇāsāṇa	,,	ṇāsāṇaṃ
	3^{b}	-o	,,	vo
	4^{9}	sajjīaṃdi	,,	sajjīanti
	4^{16}	dīsaha	,,	dīsadha
	7^{2}	jaha	,,	jahā
	16^{4}	ṇivediaṃ	,,	ṇivedidaṃ
	20^{4}	kaïṃjalo	,,	kaviñjalo
	20^{29}	lahaï	,,	lahadi
	20^{33}	karei	,,	karedi

But in spite of this the Southern recension, though very rarely, preserved some older or original forms, e.g.

I. 14^{2} Kaṇṇa (aṇṇa) suvaṇṇa° *for* jaccasuvaṇṇa

Thus we may conclude that the Southern recension is less authentic than the Northern one, though in some rare cases it may have accidentally retained what may be considered the right reading.

8. As for the Northern recension we need not discuss severally all the mss. of this class. From a study of the first twenty-five cases in which *seven* or *more* mss. (which otherwise differ among themselves) agree as regards the presence or absence of a reading we can make a very dependable estimate of the relative antiquity and

1. The final Anusvāra in fact represents the nasalization, and its disappearance in the subsequent age can easily be assumed (see below § 19).

probable authenticity not only of the Northern but also of the Southern recension as well.

I.	1^{a}	bhodu	ABPWNOR T
	1^{c}	Māgahī	ABPW STU
	2^{b}	°ghaṇa°	ABPW ORS
	4^{a}	°ppasāda°	ABPWNO STU
		°ppaṇadisu	ABPWNOR
	4^{b}	pūridāc	A PWNOR T
	4^{4}	iarā	BPWNORS U
	4^{7}	esa	AB WNOR T
	4^{10}	*om.* suṇiadi	ABPWNOR
	4^{16}	sūtradhāraḥ	A PW O STU
	5^{a}	edaṃ	A PWNORSTU
	6^{2}	sakkaaṃ	BPWNORSTU
	8^{a}	ccia	ABPW RSTU
	10^{1}	sūtradhāraḥ	BPWNOR TU
	11^{a}	mauli(maüli)	ABPWNORSTU
	11^{b}	°medami°	ABPWNORS U
	12^{b}	pariṇedi	A PWNOR T
	12^{1}	*om.* sthāpakaḥ	ABPWNOR
		bhāva ehi	ABPWNOR
	14^{a}	gade	ABPWNOR
	14^{b}	īsīsi	B WNORSTU
	14^{2}	avamaṇṇia°	BPWNORSTU
	14^{3}	iha hi	BPWNORSTU
	16^{a}	jādaṃ	ABPWNORSTU
	16^{3}	*om.* devī	ABPWNO S U

The result of the above study can be gathered in the following :

P	agrees	with	W	and	five	other	mss.	23	times
O	,,	,,	,,	,,	,,	,,	,,	23	,,
B	,,	,,	,,	,,	,,	,,	,,	21	,,
N	,,	,,	,,	,,	,,	,,	,,	21	,,
R	,,	,,	,,	,,	,,	,,	,,	21	,,
A	,,	,,	,,	,,	,,	,,	,,	19	,,
T	,,	,,	,,	,,	,,	,,	,,	16	,,
S	,,	,,	,,	,,	,,	,,	,,	15	,,
U	,,	,,	,,	,,	,,	,,	,,	15	,,

Now we have seen before (§7) that the Southern mss. STU, as regards their age, are the youngest on account of their having the most developed forms in certain words. And according to Konow W and B are relatively old among the Northern (Konow's Jaina) mss. (p. xxv). Thus we have W and B as being older than the rest of mss. used by Konow. Of these two, B however is dated later than W. Hence W becomes our oldest ms. Now we are to consider along with this the other fact that the readings (or absence of readings) with reference to which we have made the preceding study, occur with a single exception in the oldest ms. W. Hence it may probably be claimed that the degree in which the different mss. agree with W may well be considered as an indicator of their relative authenticity, and probably also of their age ; that is, P and O which agree with W 23 times are more authentic than B, N and R which agree with this only 21 times. The authenticity of A is still less, for it agrees with W only 19 times. The inferior value of the Southern mss. ascertained by another means (see § 7) has been corroborated here ; for none of them agrees with the oldest ms. W more than

16 times. And this last figure is the indicator of its inferiority to the mss. of the Northern recension. Thus we may say without any hesitation that *W is the best among the mss. used by Konow*. As no ms. older and better than this is available we shall use this as the basis of the present edition.

9. After having some more or less accurate idea of the relative worth of the mss. used by Konow we may proceed to an examination of the additional materials that have been used for the present edition. Now from the nature of our mss. this becomes an easy task. For none of these eight newly consulted mss. are in any way unique. It has been possible to find, among those used by Konow, mss. very closely resembling them. For example, the ms. D resembles the ms. O of Konow. and the ms. G has similarity to Konow's N, while the ms. I seems to have a very substantial agreement with the ms. R. As for the five Southern mss. they agree mostly with T and U used by Konow. The points in which the new mss. D G I etc. vary do not add to our knowledge of the text. From these data one can easily ascertain their relative worth, which is practically nothing.

10. *Principles of Reconstruction.* Any discussion about the principles which should be followed in editing a Pkt. work divides itself into two parts : the one, general, and the other, particular. The general part is to deal with facts which should be taken into consideration in applying the accepted canons of textual criticism to Pkt. works, and the particular part is to treat in detail the mutual disagreement between mss., doublet readings occurring in each of them and such other aspects that they may present. A wholesale inaccuracy of the Pkt. mss. as well as carelessness of Indian editors have often

been postulated by Pischel and other scholars. The grounds of their assumption are : (i) the readings of mss. often violate the rules of ancient Pkt. grammars ; (2) and in the case of Pkt. passages occurring in plays, the distinction between different dialects seem occasionally to have been disregarded. A typical instance of the latter charge is to be met with in connexion with Konow's conjectural emendation of the verses of the KM. He as well as his guru Pischel and other scholars believed that in Indian plays Pkt. verses have always been in the Mahārāṣṭrī dialect[1]. Though the early mss. of the KM. had in the clearest manner given the verses in Ś., Konow did not care to examine the age and authenticity of the socalled old tradition about the assignment of M. to versified Pkt. passages of a drama. While editing the Pkt. verses of the Bharata-Nāṭyaśāstra and Bharata's observation on Pkt. occurring in it, the present writer was brought face to face with the question ; and after his careful investigation, it turned out that the above-mentioned tradition about the use of M. does not occur in the Nāṭyaśāstra, the oldest extant work on the subject, and it does not even occur in the Daśarūpaka which is slightly anterior in time to the KM[2].

Hence, there being no positive evidence about the existence of this tradition at his time we should have no

---

1. A. Hillebrandt was probably the first scholar to produce evidence affecting such a view, but he too was a believer in it in a modified manner (see his Mudrārākṣasa, Breslau, 1911 ; Neudruck, 1935, p. iii).

2. There is however in the Daśarūpaka a passage which may be interpreted as giving support to the tradition of using M. for the verses in a drama. But it has been shown elsewhere (§21) that such an interpretation is wrong. (see Mahārāṣṭrī, p. 19).

reason to believe that Rāj. used M. in the metrical portions of his KM. Evidence of the mss. goes very strongly to support our view in the matter. We have already seen that, according to Hemacandra's definition of a saṭṭaka, the KM. could not have been composed in more languages (bhāṣā) than one (see § 2). All this very clearly demonstrates the soundness of the accepted cannon of textual criticism which is for placing greater reliance on the ms. that can be considered the best on the ground of its age as well as its degree of accuracy.

11. The postulate that the Pkt. mss. which go against the ancient grammars are corrupt is based on a very erroneous assumption, viz., the Pkt. grammars have the same binding force on the Pkt. literature as the Skt. ones on the Skt. literature. The cases of the grammars of the two languages are entirely different. Skt. grammar had its origin in priestly circles, and the accuracy of speech which they aimed at establishing or maintaining was demanded primarily in connexion with the performance of Vedic rituals[1]. Hence the study of Skt. grammar was given from very ancient times an attention quite unique in the history of human culture. But the case of the Pkt. grammars was different. Pkt. was the current language of every day use, and hence its control, even when it was given the dignified status of a vehicle of literature, was out of question, and for obvious reasons such rules were composed only very late. Thus we do not meet with great ancient names like Pāṇini, Kātyāyana

---

1. See the introduction of the Mahābhāṣya, rakṣārthaṃ Vedānām adhyeyaṃ Vyākaraṇam, ed. Kielhorn, vol. I, p. 1 ; ārtvijīnaḥ syām ity etad adhyeyaṃ Vyākaraṇam, *ibid.* p. 3.

and Patañjali in the field of Pkt. grammar. Caṇḍa (? 300 A.C.), Vararuci (? 600 A.C.), Kaccāyana (? 800 A.C.) and Hemacandra (1100 A.C.) come comparatively late, and their works can in no way bear comparison with the performance of the Three Sages (Tri-muni). And by no means should this be considered disparaging to these grammarians ; for, the circumstances under which they had to work have been considerably different from those in which the Skt. grammarians wrote. In the Brahmanic circles the study of Pkt. was scarcely encouraged. For in the Garuḍa-purāṇa (Pūrva, 98, 17) there is a passage which exhorts Brāhmaṇas, Kṣatriyas and Vaiśyas to avoid among other things Pkt[1]. Hence Pkt. was cared for by Jains and Buddhists only. But they did not care for preserving intact the linguistic form of their ancient texts, as did the Brāhmaṇas, by means of Śikṣā (phonetics) and Vyākaraṇa (grammar). It may therefore be assumed *a priori* that Pkt. grammars were written late to meet some very limited practical need, such as the understanding of old Pkt. works, be they Jain canonical works and old dramas, or the composing of the new Pkt. poems or plays, and as such they had probably to be based on those texts only which were accessible to their respective authors. A typical instance of such limited knowledge has been displayed by Vararuci, whose sūtras do not give us any information about the Pkt. of Aśvaghoṣa's drama or of the Kharoṣṭhī Dhammapada or of the Jain canons, while Paiśācī, used in no available work, has been treated in them. Hence it is no longer possible to retain an absolute and unqualified faith in the exhaustiveness and infallibility of the Pkt. gram-

1. lokāyataṃ kutarkaṃ ca Prākṛtaṃ mlecchabhāṣitam /
na śrotavyaṃ dvijenaitad adho nayati tad dvijam //

marians though Pischel was always ready to regard them with utmost confidence (see Grammatik, §§ 42f)[1]

12. Apparently such a view may be said to render impossible a critical edition of a Pkt. work, the mss. of which are very often not only in mutual disagreement with one another but also have internal inconsistency in themselves as regards the orthography and other matters. Such a condition of mss. is indeed discouraging in the beginning ; but if one follows the accepted principles of textual criticism, which require to find out the best ms. (when such is available) and to reconstruct the text on its basis, one will have enough reason to be optimistic. Disagreement of other mss. with the best one as well as a want of accord between each other of these will, with a few negligible exceptions, appear to him then to be not due to any mistake, while the internal inconsistency in each of them will often represent things other than scribal errors. Let us clear these points by quoting suitable examples from the KM.

13. We have already shown (§ 8) by referring to Konow's opinion how he has in a way considered W to be the best among the mss. of the Northern (Konow's Jaina) recension and by discussing along with this, his various readings from different mss. it has been concluded that W can be considered the best among the

1. This attitude, however, landed him at times in curious difficulties. For example when two grammars were found to differ he had to accept almost arbitrarily the testimony of one and to repudiate the other, much to the detriment of his wholesale regard for the Pkt. grammar as a class. (See IHQ. vol. VIII, no. 4, supplement, pp. 6f.).

eleven mss. utilised by Konow for his edition. We are discussing below some passages with various readings from different mss. to demonstrate further the great worth of the ms. W.

The following is a passage in the KM. (I. 20[6]) occurring in different mss. used by Konow as follows :

W	kavvaṃ	jjeva	de	kavittaṇaṃ	pisuṇedi
B	kathidaṃ	„	„	„	
A	kavvaṃ	„	„	kaïttaṇaṃ	
N	„	„	—	„	
P	„	yyeva	—	„	
O	„	jevva	de	„	
R	„	jjevva	—	„	
SU	„	evva	—	„	pisuṇei
T	kaḥ pakaḥ vaṃ	evvaṃ	de	kaïttaṇaṃ	„

13a. Let us take the variants of each word one by one. B. k a t h i d a ṃ for k a v v a ṃ in the best ms. and almost all the rest is evidently due to a later emendation. T. k a ḥ p a k a ḥ v a ṃ is evidently an error.

J j e v a occurring in four mss. including the best one is the correct reading though Pischel will not allow the doubling of j after an anusvāra (Grammatik § 95)[1]. A wrong idea about the phonetic value of the Pkt. anusvāra is responsible for this view. For the vowel with anusvāra following it, as we shall see later on (§19), is a nasal vowel and has a short quantity in Pkt. except where metre demands otherwise.

The reading STU. e v v a (ṃ) is evidently a simplified form. Readings P. y y e v a , O. j e v v a and R.

---

1. In this matter A. Hillebrandt follows Pischel in his Mudrarākṣasa, Breslau, 1911, Neudruck 1935.

j j e v v a are all traceable to j j e v a. As for the development of v a into v v a we shall discuss it later.

D e is a word though existing in the best ms. and two others, can be taken for an interpolation. For it can well be left out without in any way injuring the sense of the sentence; besides this, as far as we can ascertain, it does not in any way embellish the expression. In view of the fact that the tendency of scribes was generally for adding to mss., we may well be sure of an interpolation here when the majority of the mss. does not record the word. This however seems to minimise the authority of our best ms. But as there are different independent mss. to check its readings, we need not lose our faith in the best ms. which, being written about five centuries after the time of Rāj. is liable to contain some interpolations or mistakes. But in course of our progress with the text we shall see that cases of bad corruption in the best ms. are not many.

WB. k a v i t t a ṇ a ṃ is evidently the original reading. We are not sure if the intervocal v in Pkt. was still pronounced in Rāj.'s days. But there can be no harm in assuming that though very weakly pronounced it was written as such in his time. Indeed the mss. AN-PORSTU have all changed k a v i into k a ï but this latter reading should not be considered to have its origin in any error. For we shall see below that in other cases too these mss. record readings which are phonetically more developed than that in the best ms. or mss. standing close to it. A systematic use of developed forms in a ms. simply gives indication of the relatively young age of itself or its prototype. These remarks in connexion with k a v i applies also to STU p i s u ṇ e i for p i s u ṇ e d i. It has been shown elsewhere that the socalled Mahārāṣṭrī is most probably a development of Śaurasenī (Mahārāṣṭrī, JDL, XXIII, 1933). This in a way finds corroboration from the cases of words discussed above. The form p i s u ṇ e d i only is allowable in Ś. Hence the reading STU p i s u ṇ e i takes us to the necessary conclusion that the prototype of these mss. came into existence at a time when the forms like p i s u ṇ e d i with its d sound existing had already gone out of use and its place was taken by p i s u ṇ e i which will be usually taken as a M. form.

14. The substitution of later forms mentioned above can be explained in two ways : by considering the stage-convention regarding the use of various languages in a play, and by assuming an influence of the speech-habit of the writers of different mss. Let us first take notice of the principle of linguistic usage in the ancient Indian stage. Though it will be out of place to discuss here the subject elaborately yet we may give here in brief important data and our conclusions regarding them. The practice of using Śaurasenī and other Pkts. in the stage arose undoubtedly at a time when Skt. could mostly be understood by the speakers of Pkt. (see Winternitz, Hist. of Indian Lit. vol. I, p. 43). The discovery of the drama-fragments of Aśvaghoṣa, which, contain an older variety of Śaurasenī and other dialects, standing nearer to Skt. than the later Pkts. of classical dramas, seems to give strong support to this view. It may also be assumed that the speakers of the later Pkts. such as the Śaurasenī used in dramas, could also grasp without much difficulty the substance of the Skt. passages in them. But the fact that Skt. held its place beside the developed Ś. was not due to its any degree of intelligibility, but because of the convention. That most of the different rūpakas and upa-

rūpakas had for their plots, stories from well-known Epics, Purāṇas, collections of folk-tales etc., and were depicted on the stage with a very elaborate and familiar code of suitable gestures (a b h i n a y a)[1] considerably slackened the demand of the audience belonging to the masses with regard to the intelligibility of the Skt. passages used in them. It may not however be assumed that the producers of such plays (s ū t r a d h ā r a s) were completely indifferent to such an intelligibility. Bound though they were by convention in the case of Skt. passages they appear to have sometimes assimilated their Pkt., as far as possible, to the current popular speech just to make the Pkt. dialects used in dramas appear like living languages. This assimilation mostly consisted of a phonetic (and hence orthographic) change, or substitution of new inflectional and conjugational forms. K a ï used in some mss. instead of the original k a v i occurring in the best ms. can thus be explained.

15. Another way of explaining the appearance of such developed forms is to assume that Pkt. being a language not bound down by grammars and lexicons, mss. of this language very easily imbibed the influence of the contemporary speech of North Indian scribes who spoke some kind of Apabhraṃśa, be it of the old, middle or late period[2]. One important aspect of this Ap. is that

---

1. For a treatment of such gestures see the N a n d i k e ś v a r a ' s Abhinayadarpaṇa edited by Manomohan Ghosh in the Calcutta Skt. Series No. V. Calcutta 1934.

2. J a c o b i has suspected similar influence of New Indian Vernaculars on the writers of Apabhraṃśa. See The Bhavisattakaha, Abhandhlung 7, 1 (p.54*).

its conjugational termination of the 3rd sing. present indicative, was *-aï*, and an occasional omission, or weakening of intervocal non-nasal stops was also a feature of this language[1]. Now in Ś. present indic. 3rd sing. termination was *-adi* and intervocal stops were less often omitted or weakened. Hence if we assume an Apabhraṃśa influence on the Pkt. mss. we can easily explain the substitution of forms like k a ï for k a v i and p i s u ṇ e i for p i s u ṇ e d i. This explanation seems to be more suitable than the preceding one ; and on accepting this, we can divide the mss. of the KM. into three following groups, according to their use of developed forms :

(a). Oldest mss. W and B which stand near the original KM.

(b). Less old than the perceding mss. are ANPOR etc. which have substituted k a ï for k a v i.

(c). Latest are STU etc. which contain besides kaï for kavi, p i s u ṇ e i for p i s u ṇ e d i read by all the rest of the mss. including the best one.

16. Let us take another passage from the KM (I. 18[10]) with its various readings.

W	aha	vā	hatthe	kaṅkaṇaṃ	kiṃ	dappaṇeṇa	
B	ahā	„	hatthammi	kaṅkaṇe	„	„	
A	aha	„	hatthe	„	„	„	
N	„	„	„	kaṅkaṇaṃ	„	„	pekkhīadi
O	„	„	„	„	„	„	lakkhijjadi

1. The socalled M. also possesses these features. But I have shown elsewhere that, M. is nothing but a development of Ś. (See Mahārāṣṭrī). Hence no wonder about it.

R	aha vā	hatthe	kaṅkaṇe	kiṃ	dappaṇeṇa	pekkhiadi
P	„ „	hatthe	kaṅkaṇaṃ	„		„
S	„ „	hatthaṃmi	kaṅkaṇe	„		„
T	„ „	„	kaṅkaṇaṃ	„		„
U	„ „	hatthammi	„	„		„

Here B. ahā is against all the rest of the mss. including the best one. Though not allowed by Pischel (Grammatik § 203), aha as a Ś. form is correct according to Hemacandra. The form h a t t h e as well as h a t t h a m m i is equally correct for Ś. though Pischel objects to this also (*ibid.* § 366a). We have shown elsewhere the untenable nature of his opinion (IHQ. vol. VIII, 1932, supplement pp. 9f). But h a t t h e in the present passage existing in the best ms. should be accepted as occurring in the original work.

The reading WNOPST k a ṅ k a ṇ a ṃ seems to be better though k a ṅ k a ṇ e is not wrong. But the passage is quite good without the introduction of Sanskritic locative absolute (bhāve s a p t a m ī) which seems very much like a later emendation. Readings like p e k k h ī a d i, p e k k h i a d i, l a k k h i j j a d i are evidently late additions by pandits who probably tried thereby to make the entire passage clearer.

Thus we see that the disagreement between different groups of mss. has not always occurred as a result of accidental mistakes, and this disagreement sometime gives clue to the relative age and authenticity of the groups of mss. in question, and may, though indirectly give assistance to the proper reconstruction of the text.

So far about the orthographic or other disagreements among the different groups of manuscripts. Besides these there are found sometimes internal inconsistencies in the mss. of Pkt. works. Let us take the case of our best ms. W.

(i) The root bhū in its present indicative 3 and 2 sing. and imperative has the following forms :

bhodi, hodi, I. 20^{43} ; IV. 3^{1}.
hoi, I. 34^{10}.
bhosi, I. 19^{5}.
bhodu, I. 1^{a}, 14^{2}, $20^{26,27}$; III. 3^{2}, 22^{6}, 23^{b}, 24^{2} ; IV. 19^{48} ;
hou, I. 8^{b} ; IV. 5^{d}.

(ii) paḍisiddhī and pāḍisiddhī both occur ;
paḍisiddhī, I. 10^{b}, 20^{33} ;
pāḍisiddhī, I. 20^{12} ; II. 10^{5} ;

(iii) tuvaṃ and tumaṃ both occur ;
tuvaṃ, I. 20^{13}, ^{25}, 34^{30} ; II. 6^{6}, 32^{1}, 42^{17}, 47^{2} ; III. 2^{1}, 34^{a}.
tumaṃ, I. 16^{1}, $19^{3,5}$, $20^{10,29}$, $34^{3,20}$; II. 11^{1}, 24^{3} ; III. 22^{d} ; IV. 20^{6}.

(iv) Original kṣ is sometimes expressed as kkh and sometimes as cch

kkh ◁ kṣ *as in* pekkha, II. 43^{5}, 44^{1} and pekkhāmi, III. 20^{19}, pekkhi-, IV. 9^{18}.
cch ◁ kṣ *as in* peccha, I. 14^{d} ; III. 32^{b}, 34^{b} ; IV. 10^{b}, pecchadu in I. 16^{3} and in pecchantīṇaṃ II. 30^{c}.

(v) Verbs in the passive voice have the following forms :

-īadi, -iasi, -īāmi I. 4^{8}, 18^{18}, 19^{7} ; $20^{14,26,33}$, $25^{7,8}$, 28^{2}, 31^{a}.
-ijjae, -ijjadi, -ijjanti I. 4^{9}, 23^{b}, 25^{8}, 32^{c}.
There appear also forms like kīradu I. 20^{40}, 25^{1}.

17a. Now this variety of forms appears very much as due to confusion. We do not know whom to hold responsible for this, and an uncertainty in the matter makes the task of the editor difficult indeed. But on looking more carefully into the matter, these fluctuating forms may not appear to be so very inconvenient. Pkt. as we know it is based on a living speech controlled by no grammar, and hence it could possess many varying forms to express the same thing. Pkt. grammars with their very copious conjugational and declensional forms will corroborate us in the matter. And it can be assumed that old and new forms existed side by side in writing and probably to some extent in the spoken language as well. From such a consideration we may accept the above-mentioned varying forms as an evidence of the living spirit of the language which was at the basis of the literary Pkt.

17b. Let us discuss below the different groups of forms (mentioned above) one after another.

(i) As for the various forms of the root b h ū in Ś. Hemacandra allows bh as well as h (IV. 269) though Pischel seems to have given his verdict against h o d u and h o d i in Ś. (Grammatik § 476). That doublets like b h o d u, h o d u existed in Ś. can be corroborated by referring to New Indo-Aryan vernaculars developing out of Ś. For example in the following Rājasthānī couplet we have b h a ï as well as h o y both tracing their origin in b h o d i :

vā́ ṣ caḍhī naṭanī kahai hota no naṭiyo koy /
mai naṭ kar naṭanī *bhai* naṭai so naṭani *hoy*[1] //

---

1. N. S v ā m ī, Rājasthān-rā Dūhā, Delhi, 1935. p. 40.

Hence it may be assumed that both the forms h o d u, h o u as well as b h o d u was used by Rājaśekhara.

(ii) The doublets p a ḍ i s i d d h ī and p ā ḍ i-s i d d h ī have been allowed by V a r a r u c i (I. 2) as well as Hemacandra (I. 44).

(iii) About t u v a ṃ in the doublets t u v a ṃ and t u m a ṃ Vr. and He. are silent, still the form tuvaṃ is a genuine development from the original tvam.

It is remarkable that mss. DE (of the Prākṛta-prakāśa) used by Cowell, read t u v a ṃ instead of t u m a ṃ in Vr.'s sūtra 'yuṣmadas taṃ tumaṃ' (VI. 26) and its commentary. DE seem to have retained here the older reading while other mss. have changed the same for t u m a ṃ a further development from tuvaṃ. As tuvaṃ together with tumaṃ occurs in the Trivendrum plays[1], and t u v a ṃ alone occurs in Aśvaghoṣa's[2] work we may assume that tuvaṃ and tumaṃ existed side by side at the time of Rāj.

(iv) kṣ>(k)kh and (c)ch. In the fragments of Aśvaghoṣa (c)ch out of kṣ is not available and in the Aśoka inscriptions it occurs only in Girnar, and on this basis it was considered a characteristic of the Western dialect. But in the Bharhut inscription kṣ>(k)kh and kṣ>(c)ch occur[3]. In the so-called Mahārāṣṭrī chapters (I—IX)

1. Wilhelm P r i n t z, Bhāsa's Prākrit, p. 29.

2. A. B. K e i t h, Sanskrit Drama, p. 88.

3. Jules B l o c h, Langue Marathe. p. 7. Prof. Bloch is for taking such forms as errors. But we cannot agree with him. The double forms probably show that both the pronunciations were current at the time of the writer and he kept both the forms side by side.

of Vararuci, too, this change has very clearly been treated as an exception. For by his sūtra ṣka-ska-kṣāṃ khaḥ (III. 29) he has given a general rule for the reduction of kṣ into (k)kh, whereas his sūtras akṣyādiṣu chaḥ (III. 30) and kṣamā-vṛkṣa-kṣaṇeṣu vā (III. 31) he merely restricts the general rule and says that in special cases kṣ may develop into (c)ch as well. Hemacandra too gives likewise his general and special rules regarding kṣ in his II. 3, 17, 18.

All these facts seem to give reasons to doubt the validity of the view held by modern scholars on the basis of inscriptions that (k)kh <kṣ characterised the East and Midland dialects of the MIA and (c)ch <kṣ those of the North-west and South-west (Jules Bloch, Langue Marathe, § 104, p. 112 and S. K. Chatterji, Bengali Language, § 259, p. 469)[1]. And this doubt is further strengthened from a study of those words of the Setubandha, which have in them development of kṣ. The evidence of New Indo-Aryan Vernaculars[2] on this point does not give us any real help, for (k)kh as well as (c)ch represent kṣ in all the dialects; and it is very difficult to be sure of their origin, assumption of interinfluence not explaining all the cases. For example, Hindi *chai* Marathi *khai* and Gujarati *khā* are all derived from

1. See Appendix for a criticism of this view, based on a discussion of relevant words occurring in the Setubandha, a poem written in M.

2. See Prof. R. L. Turner's study of the distribution of the two typical developments of *kṣ* in connection with Skt. *ākṣeti* and Pali *acchati* in Modern Indo-Aryan. Bulletin of the School of Oriental Studies, London, Vol. VIII, 1936, p. 767.

OIA *kṣaya*. (Sir George A. Grierson, On the Modern IAV. § 178, p. 94). Here according to the modern theory about the geographical distribution of (k)kh and (c)ch from kṣ we are to assume that Hindi borrowed the word *chai* from the West and Marathi and Gujarati borrowed *khai* and *khā̃* respectively from the Midland. But this seems to be very confusing. Hence in the absence of any very conclusive data to support the view referred to above we may not interfere with forms like pecch- and pekkh- both from prekṣ in W.

(v) In the case of various passive forms too we may assume the existence of doublets or triplets.

It may, therefore, be not wrong to credit Rāj. himself with these, and hence,

(a) W will be considered the best ms. and it will form the basis of our reconstructed text. Its readings will not be given up except for very strong reasons ; and

(b) doublets or triplets occurring in the best ms. will not be reduced to a single form.

18. Acceptance of these principles will create for us some difficulties. For example, the best ms. has ya-śruti in some places[1]. To be consistent, we are to accept this ya-śruti too. But on account of such ya-śruti occurring

---

1. Similarly the ms. G used for S. P. Pandit's edition of the Vikramorvaśī (Bombay, 1901) and mss. SNDRI used for Pischel's edition of the Abhijñāna-śakuntala (Kiel, 1876) however record ya-śruti in quite a number of cases. About his ms. G, S. P. Pandit writes : 'it appears . . . to be about two hundred years old, possibly older. So far as it goes it is very correct' (Critical Notice, p. 1). And according to Pischel his ms S is the oldest ms. of the Bengali recension and N is a good ms.

in the ms. fragments of the Bhagavatī (a Jain canonical work) Weber considered this to be one of the exclusive characteristics of Jain Pkts. (Ueber ein Fragment der Bhagavatī, aus dem Abhandlungen der Koengl. Akademie der Wissenschaft zu Berlin, 1865 pp. 397f). But in the use of the ya-śruti Jain mss. follow no uniform practice. For example, in the mss. of the Kalpa-sūtra and the Acārāṅga used by Jacobi for his critical edition of these works he has noticed erratic practice in this matter (see the Kalpa-sūtra, Leipzig, 1879, pp. 20, 21; The Ācārāṅga-sūtra, London 1882, p. xv).

Hemacandra in his grammar (I. 180) has prescribed ya-śruti after a and ā, but in his commentary he has said that occasionally it is seen elsewhere also. Now his rule is partially confirmed by some mss. i.e. they have the ya-śruti after a and ā only, while many mss. have ya after i, ī, u, ū, e and o too. On this state of affairs Jacobi comments: "From an etymological point of view, it is more self-consistent that ya-śruti should be written after all vowels because it is the remnant of a lost consonant" (Kalpasūtra, p. 21). Now according to this very sound view even if such has not been expressly held by Vararuci and ya-śruti does not usually occur in most of the mss. of dramas, it should not be considered a linguistic feature characterizing the Jain Pkts. alone[1]. Pischel in his second part of Hemacandra's Pkt. Grammar (published in 1880) remarked (notes to sūtra I, 180) as follows:

---

1. Dr. L. Alsdorf also seems to take ya-śruti merely as a characteristic of Jain mss. Der Kumārapālapratibodha, Hamburg, 1929, p. 52, § 2.

H.'s beschraenkung des eintritts des *y* scheint mir für des Jain-prākrit nicht richtig; ich stimme darin mit Eduard Müller überein. Die Jain-handschriften haben es namentlich auch nach *i*, *ī* fast durchweg und diese ausdehnung haben es des gebrauches erhannt auch eine śikṣā bei Mārkaṇḍeya an: // anādāv aditau varṇau paṭhitavyau yakāravad // iti pāṭha-śikṣā.

Thus we see that Pischel too once expressed his view against restricting ya-śruti to the Jain Prakrit alone, though later on in his Pkt. grammar he considered it as a characteristic of the same Jain Pkt. (see Grammatik, §§45, 187). It should however be remembered in this connexion that K r a m a d ī ś v a r a who was not a Jain, prescribed ya-śruti for all Pkt. dialects (*ibid.* § 187). Hence we can well allow ya-śruti to all Pkts. where intervocal stops have been elided.

The New Indo-Aryan vernaculars also having the ya-śruti in their numerous tadbhava words give us sufficient ground to assume the existence of ya-śruti in all kinds of Pkt. from which those words have come down (see S. K. Chatterji, *op. cit.* § 170, pp. 838 ff. Sir George A. Grierson, An Introduction to the Maithili Dialect of the Bihari Language as spoken in North Bihar, pt. 1[2], Grammar, Calcutta, 1909, § 24, pp. 9-11; Pandit Hazari Prasad Dwivedi, "Hindī Ya-śruti-kī Parīkṣā", Mādhurī, vol. 9, 1988 Vikram Saṃvat, pp, 527f). Along with this should be noted the fact that in Pali too ya-śruti sporadically appears (see Geiger, Pali Lit. and Spr. § 36). Hence words occurring with ya-śruti in the ms. W can be maintained in their original form in the reconstructed text. But this procedure requiring emendatian of many words where ya-śruti does not occur (but can be expected), we have not adopted this. It may be hoped that this will not in any way diminish the usefulness of the text.

19. Another difficulty that may arise from the acceptance of W, is that it does not use the so-called anunāsika sign (ँ) and always uses anusvāra instead of this. On account of an absence of this in the mss. used by him Konow questions Rājaśekhara's linguistic skill (p. 203). But it seems that such an opinion was expressed without sufficient consideration. W h i t n e y (Skt. Grammar, §§ 70ff) has made a very elaborate discussion about the nature of ansuvāra on the basis of Pāṇini and the Prātiśākhyas of different Vedas,[1] and has concluded that the two (the anusvāra and the anunāsika) are doubtless originally and properly equivalent, and the anusvāra is a nasal sound lacking that closure of the organs which is required to make a nasal mute or contact-sound and in its utterance there is nasal resonance along with some degree of openness of the mouth (*ibid.* § 70). This statement is to some extent supported by the Śikṣā ascribed to Pāṇini (23, Ṛk recension). These views of Whitney on anusvāra though not accepted by W a c k e r n a g e l (Altindische Grammatik, I. Lautlehre, § 223) seem to be very sound and explain better the following facts :

(i) It is a very common feature of the Pkt.[2] especially Apabhraṃśa mss. to use anusvāra for the so-called

1. For the phonetic value of the anusvāra in the Prātiśākhyas and the Śikṣās see Siddheshwar V a r m a, Critical Studies in the Phonetic Observations of Indian Grammarians, pp. 148ff.

2. In Pkt, and Ap. mss. the nasal element of a consonant group including a nasal consonant seems to be often expressed by an anusvāra. Some scholars especially Jacobi is for assumming this and for substituing for such an

anunāsika (̐) sign (see Jacobi, Bhavisattakaha, Abhandlung, p. 23* and Sanatkumāracarita, Einleitung, p. XXXI ; Ludwig Alsdorf, Kumārapālapratibodha, pp. 52, 53, §4).

(ii) In the tadbhava element of the Hindi, anusvāra after a long vowel, even before a mute consonant denotes not a consonant but a nasalization, e.g. *'somṭha'* pronounced *'sõṭh'* not *'sonṭh'*, *'cāmda'* pronounced *cā̃d* and not *cānd* etc. (see Kellog, A Grammar of the Hindi Language[2], pp. 14, 549).

All this however does not clear our difficulty about the anusvāra which can be considered to be the nasalization of the vowel it follows. For in Skt. a vowel with an anusvāra is always long while in Pkt. and Apabhraṃśa versification we optionally have short or long quantity in short vowels with anusvāra. Jacobi in his critical editions of the Bhavisattakaha and the Sanatkumāracarita has used the so-called anunāsika against the anusvāra sign (of the mss.) for the cases which required to be read with a short quantity, but has retained the anusvāra (ṃ) for all cases which do not have such requirments (see Bhavisattakaha, p. 23* and Sanatkumāracarita, p. XXXI.).

anusvāra the nasal consonant of the group to which the following consonant belongs, i.e. for paṃka (ms.) Jacobi will write paṅka. We are not sure whether this is altogether correct for Ap. What is the bar to its being pronounced as pã ka ? For such pronunciation see Alsdorf, *op. cit.* p. 53. Side by side with this existed a pronunciation in which anusvāra existed as a reduced nasal. For we know that the tadbhava element of the N I A which developed out of it is pā̃k. Cf. Sir George A. Grierson, On the Modern IAV. §§103, 215 ; in §271 he thinks that ṃ is a wrong mode of indicating nasalization.

But such a distinction was not necessary to one who was a clever reader of Pkt. poetry. (We may remember here the Arabic writing with no vowel sign). Want of cleverness in this matter among other things was probably a ground of censure with speakers of living Pkts. Hāla writes. *amiaṃ pāua-kavvaṃ paḍhiuṃ souṃ-a je ṇa jāṇanti...te kahaṃ ṇa lajjanti* (I. 2.). But in spite of this kind of remarks Pkts. gradually ceased to live and hence length of short vowels with anusvāra required to be precisely indicated. This gave rise to the so-called anunāsika (̐). Jacobi however thought that anusvāra and anunāsika were two different kinds of sound and hence should be represented by two different signs. We have given above the view of Whitney which contradicts the conclusion of Jacobi. It is now plain that the Pkt. writers considered the short vowel with anusvāra to be as good as a pure vowel having a variable quantity. That the vowel with an anusvāra is as good as a pure vowel in the Ṛk Veda has been partially admitted by the Ṛkprātiśākhya (Whitney, Skt. Grammar, § 71 d). If we can accept the Pkt. vowel with an anusvāra to be like a pure vowel we may optionally give it short or long quantity according to the dictum of the Prākṛta-paiṅgala (ed. BI. 8). The soundness of this view is corroborated by the tradition among the Hindi-speaking Pandits who style the so-called anunāsika, or candra-bindu (̐) as a r d h ā n u - s v ā r or half-anusvāra[1] (Pandit Hazari Prasad Dwivedi of Santiniketan has kindly brought this fact to my notice). This term as I subsequently discovered has been used in the mss. CD, of Caṇḍa's Prākṛtalakṣaṇa exactly in this sense (see the edition of the work by R. Hoernle, p. 45.).

1. The Malayalam-speaking Pandits too have the same name for the candra-bindu (̐).

From this we can gather that the anusvāra, after the introduction of this new term very late towards the beginning of the New Indo-Aryan period (c. 1100) or even later, was set apart for the long nasalized vowels while the ardhānusvāra was used for the short nasalized ones. It seems that the Pkt. orthography never cared for the quantity of the short vowel, followed by an anusvāra though short as well as long quantity[1] obtained optionally among the Pkt. speakers.

Hence we need not question the use of anusvāras in the ms. W for indicating short as well as long nasalized vowels[2]. Similar indifference to details on the part of the Pkt. and Apabhraṃśa writers is also seen in their use of same letters of the alphabet for expressing the short and long varieties of e and o.

The initial n, and intervocal -nn- occurring in our ms. W do not find the sanction of Vararuci, and Hemacandra too does not allow them except for the Jain Pkt. Ardhamāgadhī. Hence we do not accept these features of the ms. W.

---

1. The anusvāra is of two kinds: final and medial. The general Pkt. tendency of shortening the original long final vowels has sometimes made the final vowel with anusvāra short, but the Pkt. rule of shortening the long vowel before a conjunct consonant made the medial vowel with anusvāra always long. For anusvāra which was a substitute for the nasal stop added to its quantity.

2. For the convenience of modern readers we have used in the reconstructed text the so-called anunāsika sign (̐) to denote the short nasalized vowels.

20. It has already been mentioned (§ 8) that the ms. W has been taken as the basis of the text reconstructed here. Hence, variants of those readings only of W, which from the testimony of other mss. appear to be unoriginal will as a rule be recorded. Variants from the newly consulted mss. will not be recorded for they are scarcely unique. The cases of Konow's emendation unsupported by any ms. will not be recorded, for they have been subjected to a general discussion (see § 2). Evident errors of scribes, substitution of *i*, and *u* for short *e* and *o* respectively as well as abbreviated writing such as *ṃ* for class-nasals will also be passed over in silence. When Konow gives his reading on the basis of some mss. including or not including W they will be indicated by K. while the readings of the remaining mss., which Konow rejected will be indicated by the name of those mss.

21. *The Language*. According to Sten Konow the KM. has been composed in two dialects of Pkt. : Ś. and M[1]. But we have already (§ 2) mentioned some facts which go against such a view. Here we shall discuss in details the principal argument that might be given in favour of changing the Ś. stanzas of the play into M. The Nāṭya-śāstra not to speak of prescribing M. for the metrical portions of a play, does not even recognize any dialect of this name (Keith, Skt. Drama, p. 336). And we find that neither Rāj. nor any writer of poetics older than he gives any place to M. in a play. Hence it may be assumed that M. had not been one of the dialects used in the

1. There is yet another view that the language of the KM. was Āvantī Pkt. mentioned in the Nāṭyaśāstra (see Ind. Ant. vol. 50, 1921. p. 8.).

stage before Rāj. wrote his play, But there occurs in the Daśarūpa of Dhanañjaya who was posterior to Rāj. by about two generations, a passage which tends to go against such an assumption. According to one interpretation the passage in question assigns in a play M. to women. But this interpretation is not right. We are discussing below the passage in question which is as follows :

Strīṇāṃ tu Prākṛtaṃ prāyaḥ Śauraseny adhameṣu ca /
Piśācātyanta-nīcādau Paiśācaṃ Māgadhaṃ tathā // II, 60.

According to one interpretation this may mean : 'Prākṛta[1] is generally (to be the language) of women, and Ś. in (= for) the characters of low rank etc.' (G. C.O. Haas, The Daśarūpa, N. Y, 1912. p, 75). This interpretation brings in M. in plays and assigns it to the entire women's speech whether it be in prose or verse[2], But even if writers of poetics later than Dhanañjaya assign M. to women's verses or rather gāthās, and in some recensions of the classical plays we find women's gāthās in M. form, the use of M. *prose* by any female character is attested neither from any play nor from any work on poetics (see IHQ., VIII, 1932, Supplement, pp, 6, 7 ; Keith, Skt. Drama, pp, 142, 212). Hence this interpretation seems to be altogether erroneous.

---

1. 'Prākṛta' in a narrow sense means the Mahārāṣṭrī dialect of Pkt. and is generally treated first of all in ancient grammars.

2. It is not clear on what evidence Keith states that in the Daśarūpa, Mahārāṣṭrī is assigned to the verses of persons who (normally) use Ś. (Skt. Drama, p, 336). There is no other passage in the Daśarūpa than the one discussed above which treats of the language to be used by different characters.

According to a second interpretation the Daśarūpa passage means : 'The dialect used in cases of women is generally Ś. and the same is prescribed also for male characters of low rank etc.[1]'. Now this interpretation explains facts much better. For Ś. is exclusively the language of women and of men of low rank in all available ancient Indian dramas. Thus we can conclude that M. had no chance of having a place in the KM , and Rāj. wrote this play entirely in Ś. ; and the testimony of the best ms. W. gives strong support to this.

22. We are discussing below the characteristics of Rāj.'s Ś. But we should again take notice of the fact that our best ms. of the play is nearly five hundred years later than the time in which it was actually composed, and hence the reconstructed text can be taken to represent approximately the original reserving mostly the essential characteristics of the dialect used by Rāj. As far as phonology is concerned we have reasons to think that in a few cases our best ms.. may not report the original state of affairs. But these could however be judged by an intensive study of the text.

Phonology. C o n s o n a n t s. The chief phonological peculiarity of Ś. as available in plays and for that matter the Ś. of other works seems to be the maximum retention (*i. e.* non-elision or non-reduction) of stop consonants. Some mss. of the KM. later than the best one seems to have occasionally (though not systematically) retained words in their full phonetic form, while the best ms. records them with elided or reduced consonants. An

---

1. Pischel probably followed this interpretation when he wrote : Ś. als sprach der Frauen nennt auch das Daśarūpa, 2. 60 (Grammatik, § 22).

attempt has been made before (§§14, 15) to explain the cause of such a change. In the reconstructed text however we have adopted the reading of the best and the oldest ms., for the fuller forms might as well be due to later emendations in a period when Pkt. became more or less a dead language. At that period the 'Sprachgefuehl' for Pkt. being lost, mss. had the chance of being emended with the help of grammars which gave very vague rules[1] regarding elision or reduction of stop consonants.

Apart from the general feature of Ś. mentioned above the following points about the Ś. sounds of the KM. merit discussion :

(i) The anusvāra developed from the final 'm' of the gen. pl. is sometimes elided in metrical passages, e. g. aṇāṅgaraïṇa = anaṅgaratīnām, ṇettāṇa = netrāṇām.

(ii) The original 'm' of the anusvāra before a vowel is sometimes restored in metrical passages (for the sake of metre), e. g. kāraṇam-atthi = kāraṇaṃ-atthi ; kumarīṇam-aṅga = kumarīṇaṃ-aṅga.

Note. This feature of the Ś. of the KM. is just a continuation of the OIA. phrasal combination.

(iii) Cases of spontaneous cerebralization sometimes occur, e. g. paḍāā = patākā ; kaḍhida = kvathita.

(iv) Intervocal 'ś' and 's' are in some few cases changed to 'h', e. g. divaha = divasa ; daha = daśa.

Note. This seems to be an instance of the so-called M a h ā r ā ṣ ṭ r i s m (See Woolner, Introduction to Pkt. ch. IV. § 27).

---

1. Bhāmaha remarks that elision is not allowed when non-elision promotes euphony (yatra śrutisukham asti tatra ṇa bhavaty eva *on* Vr. II. 2).

(v) Initial 't' is changed to 'c', in the word ciṭṭha di = tiṣṭhati.

(vi) Initial consonants of enclitics when they are not after an anusvāra are treated as medial ones, e. g. avi-a = api-ca ; ko-uṇa = kaḥ-punaḥ.

(vii) 'Y' of the word yaṣṭhi changes to 'l' giving rise to laṭṭhi.

Note. Mārkaṇḍeya a Pkt. grammarian of the 17th century is expressly against recognizing laṭṭhi to be a Ś. word (yaṣṭhyāṃ laś ca na syāt). But Hemacandra (12th century) sanctions such a form for Ś. (I. 247), and his opinion has certainly more weight than that of Mārkaṇḍeya who came about four centuries after the latter. (See Pkt. Verses of the Bharata-Nāṭyaśāstra, IHQ., vol. VIII, 1932, Supplement, p. 10). Sten Konow seems to think otherwise (see pp. 202f)[1]. (Linguisticians however suggest a different origin for laṭṭhi).

(vii*a*) The termination '-di', '-du' of the present indicative and imperative 3rd person singular, often appear as -i, -u ; see notes on deu (p. 1. l. 9).

Note. Elision of 'd' in such cases occurs in Bhavabhūti as well (see Todar Mall, The Mahāvīracarita p. xxxviii) and has been considered to be due his confusing of two Pkt. Ś. and M. (*ibid*).

(viii) Compound Consonants. Kh (kkh) as well as ch (cch) from kṣ, occurs in Ś. of the KM. On the strength of Mārkaṇḍeya, Pischel and Konow would like to see kh (kkh) restricted to Ś. but

---

1. A similar view has been expressed, though on a different ground, by Dr. Truman Michelson. See JAOS, vol 41, 1921. p. 462.

older grammarians do not countenance such a view which has been discussed before (§ 17b, iv). Mss. especially the older ones always allow in all dialects of Pkt. both the developments kh (kkh) and ch (cch). Pischel would, however, blame in such cases the "Ueberlieferung" of the mss. (Grammatik § 317). But this view appears to be no longer tenable.

Note. 1. In Bhavabhūti's Mahāvīracarita too we come across 'cch' as well as 'kkh' for 'kṣ' e. g. pecchijjanta (p. 51. l. 1.) and pekkha (p. 56. l. 3.). The editors have not taken notice of the fact.

Note. 2. Mārkaṇḍeya too does not give any general rule restricting kh (kkh) and ch (cch) to particular dialects.

(ix) V o w e l s. Of the various developments of the vowel 'ṛ', 'i' and 'u' (after labials) have been assigned to Ś. and 'a' has been reserved for Mahārāṣṭrī, Ardhamāgadhī, Pali and Girnar Asokan (R. L. Turner, The Position of Romani in Indo-Aryan, § 8 ; J. Bloch, Langue Marathe, § 31 ; S. K. Chatterji, Origin and Development of the Bengali Language, § 173). Of this assumed dialectal division on the basis of the development of 'ṛ' ancient Indian Pkt. grammarians are silent, In the Ś. of the KM. and in classical dramas too, we find all the developments of this sound, e, g, kada =kṛta, kidi=kṛti diṭṭhi= dṛṣṭi ; puṭṭha=pṛṣṭha ; sarisa= saḍisa=sadṛśa. This phenomenon is accounted for by assuming a mixture of dialects,

Note. In the Mahāvīracrita be find kadà (p. 46, l, 1. kadanta (p. 155, l, 7) and kida occurs in very late mss. of the work (see v.l, of kada in Todar Mall's edition). It may be mentioned here that in Pischel's first edition of the Śakuntalā there were forms like maa (=mṛga), kada (=kṛta) which have been changed by him to mia and kida in the second edition (See pp. 250ff. of the Harvard editon of the Śakuntalā).

(x) Sometimes the diphthongs 'ai' and 'au' are represented as 'aï' and 'aü.' e,g, Bhaïravāṇanda[1] = Bhairavānanda, maüli=mauḥ

(xi) Short 'e' and short 'o' non-existent in Skt, are available in Ś. The final vowel coming after a long penultimate vowel is optionally short: e. g. Sarassaïe= Sarasvatyai, aṅgaṇāo=aṅgaṇāḥ,

(xii), Lack of vowel-sandhi in a compound word is sometimes noticeable: e., g. puṇṇimā-indu.

22a. Sten Konow has assumed that the KM. was written in two dialects of Pkt., Ś. and M., and of these the latter was used in the metrical passages. It has already been shown (§ § 2, 21) that such an assumption was unwarranted and the KM. was written solely in Ś. But Rāj'.s Ś. when tested by the Pkt. grammar of Mārkaṇḍeya, is found to be incorrect (see Konow, pp. 202-203). This is the reason why Konow has concluded that 'Rājaśekhara's linguistic skill was not so remarkable as he likes to tell us.' (*ibid* p. 203). We have pointed out before (§ § 1, 11)

---

1. Mss. of the KM. except SU have Bhairavāṇanda. That no ms. reads Bheravāṇanda and SU read Bhaïra° is the reason for assuming the form Bhaïravāṇanda. The Pkt. 'aï' sounded shorter than the Skt. 'ai', and it was something like the 'ai' of Modern Hindī (See Sir George Grierson, On the Modern IAV, § 110). Pischel quotes Mārkaṇḍeya's view to say that the Skt. 'ai' does not occur in Ś, a 'ai'. See Grammatik § 61.

the inherent defect of the assumption which seeks to correct Pkt. texts with the help of the Pkt. grammarians' dicta. This disposes of Konow's claim of testing Rāj.'s Ś. by the grammar of Mārkaṇḍeya. And we may conclude that Rāj's linguistic skill was not as so defective as Konow likes us to believe (*loc. cit*). Occasional use of developed or so-called M. forms like -i,. jahā., jaha, iha (besides the fuller forms -di, jadhā and idha) in the KM. even if they were not due to late scribes, should not be made a ground for reproaching Rāj. with an ignorance of the characteristics of different Pkt. dialects. For all we know Ś. does not seem to be genetically different from M. and Rāj's usage in a way support the view that M. is a late phase of Ś[1]. If he has sometimes used developed forms instead of uniformly using archaic ones and thus has not made his composition look exactly. like Ś. of early dramas we may think that he was writing merely to give aesthetic pleasure to an audience and not fabricating a document of archaic Pkt. That he could write some sort of Ś., accurate enough to give such pleasure amply justifies his claim of being 'one skilled in all languages' (*savva-bhāsā-cadura*). This way of looking to it may however lessen the value of the KM. as a document of Pkt. But we should consider the fact that Rāj. being in all probablity a speaker of some sort of Early New Indo-Aryan was not in a position to give us the Ś. of classical plays, which was by that time a dead language. Hence any assumption about the great value of the KM. as a document of Pkt. was fundamentally wrong (cf. Konow. p. 203). The KM. is evidently a late Pkt. work and as such its testimony on Pkt. is inferior to

1. See Mahārāṣṭrī, JDL. XXIII. 1633.

that of the classical plays by Kālidāsa, Śūdraka, etc. That the KM. contains a number of deśī words, much larger than that occurring in any such classical play, is one of its late features. Developed forms if they have been actually used by Rāj. can be considered another of such feature.

23 *The Original Feature.* The KM. has been one of the few plays written entirely in Pkt. and as such it has a special claim to our attention. This exclusive use of Pkt. by all the characters in a play has not however been sanctioned by the Bharata-Nāṭyaśātra (c. 500 A. C. in its present form) which is the earliest available authority on the subject. Nor does the Daśarūpa of Dhanañjaya who was younger than Rāj. by about two generations mentions saṭṭaka or any kind of play in which Pkt. alone is to be used. (Dhanika however quotes in his Avaloka on the DR. a passage from the KM. but he never mentions saṭṭaka in his commentary). Thus we may well assume that this rather unconventional use of Pkt. for the entire play was an original idea with Rāj.[1]

But before we can give him any credit for this bold innovation we must try to find out what artistic purpose it served. Besides the KM. Rāj. wrote three or more plays and in them he adhered to the rules given in the NŚ. about the assignment of Skt. and different dialects of Pkt. to different characters. Can it be said that the KM. just because of its language, is more excellent than other plays? No, Rāj. was well aware of the fact and he seems to have anticipated the criticism of the upholders of con-

1. The word saṭṭaka is said to occurr in the form of sāḍaka in the Bharhut inscriptions (Konow. p. 195). But sāḍaka does not probably mean a drama. It might as best have meant a kind of dance in which six members took part.

vention in the matter. To explain his position he puts in the mouth of the sūtradhāra the question: "Then why has the poet abandoned the Skt. language and undertaken a composition in Pkt.?" and answers the same in the person of the pāripārśvika by saying that, "a poem is a peculiar way of expression, be the language whichsoever it may." (The passage about Pkt. being sweeter than Skt. is spurious. On this see Notes). This however seems to be avoiding the real answer in a very clever way. The very fact that Rāj. quite against the convention used Pkt. for the entire play shows that he had some very weighty reason behind the step. Now can this be merely for the display of his linguistic ability? For did he not mention himself as an expert in all languages (savvabhāsā-cadura)? It has already been mentioned that in the KM. Rāj. used only Śaurasenī; hence we cannot assume that he wrote this to show his skill in using different languages. (cf. Konow, p. 203).

The real reason behind the innovation seems to be Rāj.'s desire for poetic experiment about which he as an artist cannot take the audience into confidence. Hence his rather evasive answer quoted above. It is possible that in his experiment Avantisundarī,[1] his talented wife, gave him hearty encouragement. For it was at her instance that the play was staged for the first time. And it is very likely that this first performance of the play took place in Rāj.'s own residence where a select gathering were invited to attend. But all this is a conjecture.

---

1. Hemacandra in his Deśīnāmamālā mentions Avantisundarī, the authoress of a Pkt. Deśīkoṣa. She may be identical with Rāj.'s wife. See Annals of the Bhandarkar Oriental Research Institute, vol. VIII, 1927, p. 64.

Whatever might be the actual condition under which the play was staged, it goes without saying that this novel play pleased the audience and it was afterwards circulated far and wide and gave rise to divergent recensions and at times readings of pretty bewildering nature.

24. All this may be said to point to its great papularity which, it is probable, was achieved partly by the beautiful dance introduced into it and partly by its exclusive use of Pkt. which was more comprehensible to the common people of those days than Skt. As for dances in the performance of the KM. we shall take up the subject later on (§ 26) and shall discuss here only how the Pkt. used in the play might have made it popular. At the time of Rāj. (*c.* 900 A. C.) speakers of Indo-Aryan languages were already using in their daily life some kind of Apabhraṃśa[1] which was going to develop in course of two or three following centuries into a more or less analytic language (an early stage of the New Indo-Aryan vernaculars). Thus it is almost sure that the common people of those days were already finding it difficult to follow Skt. in prose or verse, though conditions were quite different some four or five centuries before Rāj. when Kālidāsa and others wrote their dramas. Ś. of the classical dramas though it had some features of a synthetic language was far simpler than Skt. and was obviously more easily intelligible to speakers of Apabhraṃśa which was then slowly developing. Hence it may be assumed that the common people of Rāj.'s time could enjoy his KM. written entirely in Pkt. better than other plays in which Pkt. was assigned a minor position.

---

1. By Ap. we mean that stage of the MIA. which came after the Pkt. of the dramas and poetical literature.

24a. *Its Literary Value.* Though Rāj. might have written his play entirely in Pkt. for making it intelligible to common people, it did not in any way lack embellishments of a Skt. dṛśya-kāvya. From his very *maṅgalācaraṇa* in which he mentions the three rītis we can assume his intention of applying all these (Vaidarbhī, Māgadhī and Pāñcālī) in the KM. And actually we see that the play has been written in an intermixture of Vaidarbhī and Pāñcālī with occasional examples of Māgadhī or Gauḍī as it has been named in the Kāvya-mīmāṃsā (p. 8) by Rāj. In his classification of rītis Rāj. agrees with that of Vāmana (*circa.* 750-825 A.C.). For Bhāmaha (*c.* 700 A.C.) and Daṇḍin (*c.* 700 A.C.) have named two rītis, Vaidarbhī and Gauḍī. To these, Vāmana has added a third, Pāñcālī, while in Rudraṭa's Kāvyālaṃkāra we meet with a fourth, Lāṭī (Nobel, Foundation of Indian Poetry, p. 123; also S. K. De, Skt. Poetics, vol. II. p. 76).

A suitable intermixture of three different rītis in the diction of the KM. has given it a varied charm which is not usually met with in the latter-day Skt. dramas. A great variety of Skt. metres including the most complicated ones like Śārdūlavikrīḍita, Vasantatilakā and Sragdharā etc. which he has used, has also given his play as a whole a delicate yet forceful rhythm which bespeaks the acute art-sense of Rāj. Indeed he has imitated his predecessors like Kālidāsa, and Śrīharṣa in building up his plot, but both in his language and character-painting Rāj. has shown considerable skill and ability (cf. Lanman, pp. xivf. and also Konow, pp. 204f.).

25. *Historical Value.* Konow writes: "The Karpūramañjarī is also of importance for the history of the Indian drama in general. To judge from some indication

in the thetorical literature, one must suppose that in early times, a sthāpaka (as well as a sūtradhāra) had to do with the arrangement of the play. But in the most known plays the sthāpaka disappeared......

In the Karpūramañjarī, we still find the sthāpaka in action" (p. 196).

He admits, however, that the most of of mss. do not support the reading sthāpaka in the place of sūtradhāra (*ibid*), and has tried to raise his suggestion to a theory by discussing the last prose passage in the prologue of the KM. (1.12^{1-3}) which is as follows ;

tā ehi aṇantara-karaṇijjaṃ sampādemha jado mahā-rāa-devīṇaṃ bhūmiaṃ ghettuṇa ajjo ajjabhāriā a javaṇinatare vaṭṭanti.

But on a reconsideration of the passage which has variant readings we are inclined to believe that it was due to a misunderstanding of the original passage that it came to be corrupted, and the corruption introduced in some mss.[1] the sthāpaka in the place of the sūtradhāra. We are giving our reasons below.

---

1. Konow does not expressly mention which mss. read sthāpaka. But from the mss. cited we can gather that the following will be a true statement of the testimony of his mss. on this point :

1.2^{1} PRT sthāpaka	ANBW	sūtradhāra, OS silent	
1.4^{15}	ANPWORSTU	"	B "
1.4^{19}	all mss.	"	
1.5^{1}, 8^{1}......................	"	"	
$1,10^{1}$ S sthāpaka	ABPWORT	"	

Of the mss. PR of the Northern recension which record sthāpaka, P was influenced by the Southern recension

Three mss. WANB including the best one uniformly put the passage in the mouth of the pāripārśvika and this, as we shall see bellow, was most probably the original arrangement. The passage seems to have been corrupted in a peculiar fashion and the mischief came most probably form a misunderstanding of the expression 'ajjā ajjabhariā-a' which occurred in the original version of the passage instead of 'ajjo ajjabhariā-a'. The interpolator who changed the entire passage considered *a* (= Skt. *ca*) as equivalent to 'and' but in fact *a* here meant 'beside'. (Our suspicion in the matter in a way finds corroboration from the ms. P which reads 'ājjā ajjabhāriā' instead of 'ajjo ajjabhāriā-a' and has the verb vaṭṭadi in the singular). Now reconstructed in the light of above mentioned facts the passage will stand thus :

bhāva[1] *ehi. aṇatnara-karaṇijjaṃ sampādemha. Jado* [2]*mahārāa-deīe bhūmiaṃ ghettuṇa ajjā*[3] *ajjabhāriā-*[4]*a javaṇiantare ciṭṭhadi*[5].

[Tr. Come sir, what we have at once to do let us

(p. xxvi). This probably shows that sthāpaka was a later insertion in the prototype of some of the Southern mss. This Southern recension is as we have seen (§7) is of inferior value. And R. on this point is suspicious too. New mss. examined especially those of the Southern recension give us enough ground for suspicion.

1. ABPWNOR bhāva ehi, CST tā ehi, A ehi dāva.

2. N mahārāassa deīe, the remaining mss. mahārāa-devīṇaṃ.

3. B appā, P ājjā.

4. P omits a.

5. W ciṭṭhaṃti, PN, vaṭṭadi, AV, vaṭṭaṃdi, T vaṭṭai, R ×ḍaḍi.

accomplish ; for her ladyship Mrs. Director is on her part in the tiring room after finishing her make-up for the role of the chief queen of the king.]

It is apparent how the interpolator has added 'ां' (āṃ) to देवीए to change it into देवीण+ां=देवीणां (devīṇaṃ) and ciṭṭhadi has been changed to ciṭṭhanti.

This we may think disposes of the view of Prof. Konow who has tried here to give support to Pischel's well-known theory of the puppet-play origin of Indian drama, which according to Keith "cannot be regarded as plausible" (The Sanskrit Drama, p. 56). We are not concerned here with the validity of this theory ; but it can be safely said that the materials are quite inadequate to find in the Karpūramañjarī any evidence in its support.

26. The KM., though it does not give us any help in studying the origin of the Indian drama, surely throws light on some minor points connected with its nature and later history. The prologue gives us a very graphic picture of the activities of Kuśīlavas at the beginning of a play. The dhruvā songs about which the Nāṭyaśāstra devotes one entire chapter (XXXII) have been mentioned here. We also learn from it the names of various musical instruments which were in use in the orchestra of the time (c. 900 A. C.). The beautiful dance which occurs in act IV. and has been described by the Vidūṣaka, illumines to some extent the usage of applying dance in the Indian stage. Besides this, the bhramarī performed by the king at the end of the play gives also similar help to the student of the Indian drama.

27. The KM. has also some importance for the religious history of India. In it occurs one of the early references of the Tāntric teachings. Bhairavānanda

wrongly taken to be a magician by Konow and Lanman was in fact a *siddha-puruṣa* of the Tāntric sect. It was believed formerly that a person who has rightly exercised himself according to the method prescribed by the Tāntric tradition not only attained a spiritual height but also developed some occult powers (*siddhis*) by means of which he could accomplish miracles. Any one who could thus work miracles in this way was called a *siddha-puruṣa.* Hence Bhairavānanda was not a magician in the ordinary sense but a *siddha-puruṣa* having attained a spiritual height as well as occult powers according to the common Indian belief. And he was first a religious teacher and incidentally a maker of miracles. Konow and Lanman have thoroughly misunderstood the character of Bhairavānanda, for Rājaśekhara cannot be said to have any grudge against this Tāntric *siddha-puruṣa* to paint him as a magician and charlatan. For in the last act we see that the queen makes him her spiritual guide (guru). If Bhairavānanda were a mere magician his acceptance by the queen as her spiritual guide would have been improper. It is not possible that Rāj. lowered her dignity by purposely making her the disciple of a sorcerer. To the general reader who will superficially read the words of Bhairavānanda on his first entrance in the act I, they will appear very improper. But they had a double meaning and have been explained in the Notes. For he showed himself as a drunken person and said certain things which are apparently vulgar and immoral. But this apparently disgusting feature of his words is a way of concealment. The inner meaning of his words will be clear from the following translation :

"I do not know any mystic formulae (*mantra*) or scriptures (*tantra*), neither any meditation had I to practice; (all this liberty was) due to the favour of my spiritual guide (guru). I shall drink, and enjoy the company of a woman (i. e. my own wife) and shall attain the salvation attached to the Kaula tradition,"

"A widow or a caṇḍāla woman I may take as my legal wife. Wine may be drunk and meat may be eaten; begging will bring me (lit. be) food, and a piece of hide will be the bed. To whom will these Kaula ways not appear as lovely ?"

"Gods like Hari and Brahman say that the salvation will come from meditation and the performance of Vedic sacrifices. Only (Śiva) the consort of Umā has seen salvation along with wine and woman."[1]

In the above translation which keeps close to the original we find nothing objectionable. For the teachings of the Tantra go against asceticism and hence a follower of this religious tradition will not admit that the company of one's wife or a moderate quantity of meat and drink will stand in the way of one's attaining salvation. Caste[2], Vedic rituals and customs also were discouraged by the followers of the Tantra. Hence Bhairavānanda said that the Tantra permitted one to take a widow or a caṇḍāla (a very low class) woman as his wife, and Vedic

---

1. Lanman's free metrical translation of these passages gives only one of their two meanings. Any one taking this translation as their only meaning will do an injustice to Rāj.'s clever composition.

2. We may remember here Rājaśekhara's marriage with a Kṣatriya lady. If Rāj. was a Brahmin then this marriage is likely to have occurred in the Tāntric from or his was the time-honoured *pratiloma* marriage.

sacrifices were not necessary for salvation. Thus we see that Bhairavānanda had a perfect method behind his pretended madness. His apparently vulgar and immoral words invested as they were with a double meaning were intended to produce some dramatic effect. All this information is very valuable for the history of Indian religion especially of the Tāntric sect.

III. RAJASEKHARA

28. *His Date.* From the evidence supplied by his dramas we learn that Rāj. was the *upādhyāya* of Mahendrapāla king of Kanauj and was also patronized by his son and successor Mahīpāla.[1] Now the Siyodani inscription informs us that Mahendrapāla reigned between 903-907 A. C. while his son Mahīpāla about 917 A. C. (Epigraphia Indica, i, p. 171). There are, besides, other data for making an estimate of Rāj.'s time. In the Kāvyamīmāṃsā he quotes, among other authors, Udbhaṭa and Ānandavardhana who flourished respectively during the reign of Kashmirian kings Jayāpīḍa (719-813 A. C.) and Avantivarman (857-884 A. C.). And he in his turn was referred to by Somadeva and Soḍḍhala (or Soṭṭhala) who flourished respectively in 960 A. C. and 990 A. C. From this it can be concluded that Rāj. lived and had his literary activities *circa* 880-920 A. C.

29. *His Place of Origin.* From the Bālarāmāyaṇa we learn that some among Rāj.'s ancestors were inhabi-

1. Prof. Konow on the ground of some epigraphic and literary references has conjectured that Rāj. at some time of his life had connexion with the Cedi court. But the name of Cedi curiously enough, does not occur in the geography of India given in Rāj.'s Kāvyamīmāṃsā (See pp. 93f.)

tants of Mahārāṣṭra. Konow has identified this country with Vidarbha nnd Kuntala (p. 180) but after the discovery of Rāj.'s Kāvyamīmāṃsā we can no longer accept this identification, for in this work Mahārāṣṭra as distinct from Vidarbha and Kuntala, has been mentioned as a part of the Dakṣiṇāpatha or the Deccan (3rd. ed. p. 93).[1] But whatever be the location of Mahārāṣṭra it appears by no means certain that Rāj. had this locality as the place of his origin, Reasons for our doubt are as follows : We all know how Daṇḍin has eulogised the Mahārāṣṭrī Pkt. But Rāj., though we know him from his works to be a great lover of Prakrit has described it as the favourite language of the inhabitants of Lāṭadeśa (Kāvyamī. p. 51) has not in any way associated it with Mahārāṣṭra. This is an occasion where Rāj. might have given us some clear indication about his assumed birthplace. It cannot be said that out of modesty he has remained silent ; for a person who boldly styles himself as the master of all languages (*sabbabhāsā-cadura*) can scarcely be credited with such weakness with regard to his native place which, if we are to believe Daṇḍin, possessed the best kind of Prakrit. Hence it becomes difficult to believe that Mahārāṣṭra was the birth place of Rāj. But this view may be objected to on the assumption that either the reputation of Mahārāṣṭra as the home of the most excellent Pkt. no longer continued, or it may be that Daṇḍin's Mahārāṣṭra (identical with Rāj.'s) was somewhere on the southern border of the Indian Midland

---

1. In the Bālarāmāyaṇa Rāj. identifies Vidarbha with Kuntala. (III. 50-52, X. 74-75). Mr. Mirashi says 'Kuntala is generally taken to refer to the Southern Maratha country'. Annals of the Bhandarkar Oriental Research Institute, Poona XI. p. 366).

(and not in the Western Deccan as supposed by Konow, see p. 180) and was linguistically indivisible from it (See M. Ghosh. Mahārāṣṭrī, esp. § 7). We have already shown the doubtful nature of the tradition recorded by Daṇḍin (*ibid*). Rāj.'s absolute silence about M. seems to give strong support to our assumption that Daṇḍin's praise of the M. was a patriotic exaggeration[1] (*ibid* § 35). From the fact that Rāj. who recorded the tastes of different kings of the past with regard to their patronization of different languages, did not mention any of the kings of Mahārāṣṭra who, if we are to believe Daṇḍin, can be excepted to have patronized the Mahārāṣṭrī Pkt. (see Kāvyamī. p. 50). On the other hand we find no data on the basis of which we can conclude that Rāj.'s indifference to Mahārāṣṭra in connection with Pkt. might be due to this country falling, at his time, from its past linguistic or cultural supremacy. Let us now discuss the second alternative. As Sir George Grierson applies the name Mahārāṣṭra to the locality lying south of the area where speeches directly descended from Śaurasenī prevail nowadays (Linguistic Survey of India, vol. VII, p. 123), it does not appear to be improbable that Mahārāṣṭra of Rāj. was contiguous to the Midland. But even then it will be difficult to connect Rāj. with Mahārāṣṭra. For he seems to have given a very clear indication about his relation to the Midland. These are as follows :

1. Mr. S.S. Ramaswami is for identifying Pravarasena the author of the Setubandha with Vākāṭaka Pravarasena. II (*c.* 405-435) the king of Kuntala. This identification will be acceptable if Mahārāṣṭra of Daṇḍin is to be considered another name of Kuntala. But Rāj. has two different countries with these two names (*Kāvyamī*, p. 93). In Vātsyāyana (*c.* 400) occur the two different names Kuntala and Mahārāṣṭra (VI, 5, 29 ; 7, 27).

(i) In the Kāvyamī. he says: yo madhyadeśaṃ nivasati sa kaviḥ sarvabhāṣā-niṣaṇṇaḥ (p. 51). (The poet who lives in the Midland is well-versed in all languages). This taken witk the fact that Rāj. calls himself a master of all languages (*sabbabhāsā-cadura*) gives grounds of presumption to have the Midland as his birth place.

(ii) He glorifed Śaurasenī, the Pkt. of Midland origin by writing one entire drama in it. (I have shown elsewhere that the term *Prākṛta* mentioned in his Kāvyamīmāṃsā can be nothing other than Ś. See Mahārāṣṭrī, § 38).

(iii) Rāj.'s partiality for Kanauj and Pañcālas too signifies more than his love and admiration for his pupil and patron both kings of Midland which had then Mahodaya (Kanauj) for its capital. He says that directions should be reckoned from this city and describes it as a very sacred place and its ladies as leaders of fashion in the matter of female dress, ornaments, speech and manners etc., for other Indian provinces (Kāvyamī. p. 8, Bālar. X, 88-90). For the Pañcālas he has a great praise (Bālar., X. 86).

From the above three points we may be nclined to believe that Mahārāṣṭra was not Rāj.'s place of origin even if this place was not the western Deccan. The traditions regarding Rāj.'s origin and his own statements and predilections may be reconciled by assuming that his ancestors came to Madhyadeśa from some place in Mahārāṣṭra.

30. *His Family*. Rāj. has given some information about himself and his family. From his Bālar. (I. 6, 13) and the Viddha. (I. 5^2) we learn that he belonged to the Yāyāvarakula. But it is not possible to gather from this whether he was a Brāhmaṇa or Kṣatriya. His marriage with Avantisundarī who was Kṣatriya lady of Cauhāna

family makes it probable that he was a Kṣatriya. But marrying a Kṣatriya should not stand in the way of his having been a Brāhmaṇa. For in those days *anuloma* marriage, i. e. marrying below one's own *varṇa* was perhaps not yet prohibited. Or it may be that Rāj. as has been conjectured by Konow was Śaiva (p. 180) and as such he could marry according to Śaiva rites wife from any *varṇa* without degrading himself in the least. But Konow, too, following Apte considers Rāj. to have been a Brāhmaṇa, because he is said to have been an incarnation of Bhavabhūti and it was unbecoming for a Kṣatriya to be a guru or upādhyāya (*loc. cit*). The first objection is not at all strong; as for the second, this too does not seem to be allowable, for the verdict of the Dharmasūtras are not against this; Rāj. might have been an upādhyāya of the king and a Kṣatriya. That Rāj.'s father Durduka was the chief minister (*mahāmātra*) of a king (Bālar. I, 13[1]), however, inclines us to believe that he was a Brāhmaṇa ; for we know of some famous Brāhmaṇa ministers viz. Cāṇakya, Sāyaṇa etc. But we have no means to be sure on this point. As Brāhmaṇas have sometimes been the chief commander of the army (senāpati), a post to which Kṣatriyas should naturally be entitled, Kṣatriyas too at times might have occupied the position of a minister. Works like the Kāmandakīya Nītisāra have not layed down any rule that Brāhmaṇas *only* would have to be made ministers.

The Yāyāvara family whether it was Brāhmaṇa or not, had a great reputation for producing men of letters. Rāj. has several times mentioned this fact. But among these literary men Akālajalada only was one of his ancestors. Surananda, Tarala and Kavirāja belonged probably to different branches of this family. The fact that Rāj. in a passage quoted in the Sūktimiktāvalī (see Kāvyamī. p. XXX) speaks of *yāyāvara-kulaśreṇī*, or series of Yāyāvara families, justifies us to hold the above view. Even if these great names did not belong to the branch of the Yāyāvara family to which Rāj. belonged his family was surely much distinguished for learning and manifold activities, for his father Durduka came to occupy the position of a mahāmātra.

31. *His Personality*. Born in such a cultured family Rāj. could receive a good education and become acquainted with different branches of the contemporary Hindu learning, From the fact of his display of great versatility in the newly discovered Kāvyamīmāṃsā we can infer all this. His enumeration, in connextion with the equipment of a poet, of the various arts and sciences in the chapter VIII of this work gives us an idea as to the liberal education of his time. Rāj. being himself a poet and applying to himself the proud title of a 'Kavirāja' who is above a 'Mahākavi' it will not be wrong to assume that he himself came up to the standard he set up for the poets and had a fair acquaintance with different branches of studies besides literature in which he was a master.

But Rāj. was not merely a scholar, He had some literary powers which have won for him a permanent, though not a very high place in the Sanskrit literature. Indeed he has freely drawn ideas, motifs, imageries etc. from his predecessors like Kālidāsa and Bhavabhūti but he has always displayed sufficient skill in assimilating them and giving on them a stamp of his own by introducing at times novel expressions. From a study of the chapters XI-XIII of the Kāvyamīmāṃsā where he discusses very elaborately the art of borrowing in course of literary compositions he shows a great deal artistic sense as well as great command over the Sanskrit language.

32. *Rājaśekhara's Works.* Four plays of Rāj. are extant, and a work on poetics by him named Kāvyamīmāṃsā has come to light a few years ago. In his Kāvyānuśāsana Hemacandra has named a poem (kāvya) of Rāj. named Haravilāsa. Thus we have altogether six works from the pen of Rāj. It is not however known for certain how many works he composed. In his prologue to the Bālarāmāyaṇa we are informed that he wrote six works most probably including that play. But as we have no reliable evidence as to the order in which his available works were composed this information may give us varying numbers of his literary productions V. S. Apte and Prof. Konow conjectured the chronological order of his works (available before 1901) as follows: Karpūramañjarī, Viddhaśālabhañjikā. Bālarāmāyaṇa and Bālabhārata. On the basis of this view Rāj.'s works would be no less than nine. There is also a view that would take the Bālarāmāyaṇa and the Bālabhārata as early productions of the poet. In pursuance of this we shall have the number of Rāj.'s works as not less than nine or ten. There is yet another view (of Mr. V. V. Mirashi[1]) which considers the Bālar. to be the earliest of Rāj.'s works and this would make the number of Rāj.'s works as not less than ten. Mr. Mirashi's view seems to be the most plausible.

From the Bālarāmāyaṇa passage it appears that the drama itself was the first play of Rāj. and he wrote before that five or six kāvyas (possibly of different types)

1. 'The Chronological Order of Rājaśekhara's Works' in Pāṭhak Commemoration Volume, Poona, 1934, pp. 359f.

and they were not very much appreciated ; for Rāj. says that even if the critics would not care to study his purely poetical works so remarkable for their clever expressions the actors would for a long time recite his (dṛśya) kāvyas threadbare. The Haravilāsa mentioned by Hemacandra must have been one of the early kāvyas of Rāj., which have been lost. This view would make the number of Rāj.'s works no less than ten.

In the chronological order of Rāj.'s works suggested below we have followed Mr. Mirashi (*loc. cit.*) as far as possible.

(*i*). *Six Early works.* Most probably they were poems to be read (śravya kāvyas = poems to be heard) and the Haravilāsa might probably have been one of such kāvyas. (*ii*). *Bālarāmāyaṇa.* This was probably the first play of Rāj. (*iii*). *Bālabhārata.* This seems to be the next production. Its alternative title Pracaṇḍapāṇḍava seems to refer to Mahīpala. Mr. Mirashi gives argument why it should be placed before the Karpūramañjarī. (*iv*). *Karpūramañjarī.* Konow took this to be the first play of Rāj. (p 184). But the circumstances under which the play was originally produced go against such a view (see Introduction § 23). (*v*). *Viddhaśālabhañjikā.* This play was written at the court of Yuvarājadeva I, who dealt a heavy blow to the declining power of the Pratihāra dynasty during the last years of Mahīpāla's reign. According to Mr. Mirashi Rāj. seems to have come back to Tripuri the home of his ancestors. (*vi*). *Kāvyamīmāṃsā.* This seems to be the production of his declining age and Mr. Mirashi thinks it was composed at the court of Tripuri. But omission of Cedi from his list of countries in this work cannot be explained on this assumption.

APPENDIX

Is the SETUBANDHA *written in Mahārāṣṭrī ?*

Ancient Hindu grammarians of Prakrit never gave any rule or rules which may be taken to prove that the Middle Indo-Aryan developments like kṣ>kh-, kkh,- kṣ>-ch,-cch- in any way determine the dialectal affinity of the language in which they occur. But modern scholars have however tried to view the matter independently, and they suggest after a study of various data that these developments indicate a dialectic division of India. According to them kṣ>kh-,-kkh- is connected with the group of dialects including AMg., Mg. and Ś., and kṣ>ch-, -cch- to M., and cases which would not admit of explanation by means of this theory are explained on the assumption that some mixture of dialects has occured. In the present note we like to test this theory on the language of the Setubandha (Rāvaṇavaha) which according to Daṇḍin has been written in M.

The following are the words from the above-mentioned Pkt. poem, in which Old Indo-Aryan kṣ has developed to either kh-,-kkh- or ch-,-cch-. (These have been collected from the glossary of G o l d s c h m i d t 's edition.)

(i) Words having *kh-,-kkh-<kṣ* : akkha (*N. pr.*); akkhara , a-rakkhasa ; ahikkheva ; ikkha (*Skt.* ikṣ) *as in* pekkhasa, pekkhijjanta, pekkhaï, paḍikkhanti, aṇavekkhia; kakkha ; kaṅkha, kaṅkhanta, kaṅkhia ; khaa ; parikkhaa ; khi *as in* khavei, khaventi, khavijjaï, khavia ; khip *as in* akkhivaï, akkhitta, samakkhettūṇa, ukkhiventi, ukkhippanti, ukkhippanta, ukkhitta, samukkhitta, parikkhitta, vikkhitta ; khubh *as in* khubbhaï, khuhia, khohenti,

khohenta, khohijjanta, khohia, ukkhohia, pakkhubbhantaa, pakkhuhia, saṃkhohia ; khaa ; khaṇa, takkhaṇa ; kheva ; khoha ; gavakkha ; cakkhu ; ṇakkhatta ; ṇikkheva ; dakkhiṇāaṇa ; dakkhiṇṇa ; dhummakkha ; pakkha, -vakkha ; paccakkhe ; parikkhaa ; parirakkhaṇa ; parokkha ; mokkha ; rakkhasa ; rakkha ; rakkha- *as in* rakkhijjaï, rakkhia, parirakkhasu, parirakkhanta ; rukkha ; lakkha (-kṣya-, -kṣa) ; -lakkha *as in* lakkhijjaï, °jjanti, lakkhei, lakkhijjanta, lakkhī, alakkhia, dullakkha ; vikkheva ; vimokkha ;-mukkha ; saṃkhaa ; saṃkhoha ; hiraṇṇakkha.

(ii) Words having *ch-,-cch-* < *kṣ*. accha (*eye*) ;-acchaa (= vṛkṣaka) ; acchi ; acchivatta (akṣi-) ; icch (*Skt.* ikṣ) *as in* pecchāmi, pecchaï, pecchanti, peccha, pecchasu, pecchaha, pecchanta, pecchiuṃ, pecchia, pecchiavva ; ucchevaṇa ; chip *as in* ucchippanta, ucchitta (*often v.l. for* °kkhi° *see also* khip. *above*), chunda (kṣud) *as in* chundati, anacchuṇa, occhuntanti °ai, occhuṇa, aṇacchuṇa ; dacchihisi, °hi , dacchāma, decchimha (?) from drakṣa ; duppeccha (= °prekṣya) ; riccha (ṛkṣa) ; lacchi, lacchia ; vaccha, vacchala.

From a study of these words we find that kh-, -kkh- < kṣ which is a non-M. feature appears in as many as 81 cases, while ch-, -cch- < kṣ which is a M. feature only in about 30 cases. Thus the number of non-M. loan-words (81) in the Setubandha which might well have had doublets with M. phonetic character (with reference to original kṣ) are much in excess of words which have actually that character.

All this tends to shaken very much our faith in the modern theory about the dialectal division of MIA on the basis of the divergent developments of the OIA kṣ. As the Setubandha has been written in M. which according to Daṇḍin was Pkt. per excellence (p r a k ṛ ṣ ṭ a ṃ p r ā k ṛ t a m) we should expect that ch, -cch $<$ kṣ would be more available in it than kh-, -kkh- $<$ kṣ; for it is always the case that a dominating literary language or dialect takes loan-words from another language or dialect, does so only very sparingly. Hence one must be very sceptical either about the value of Daṇḍin's testimony about the language of the Setubandha or the theory of dialectic division based on the development of kṣ. If however we like to adhere to the modern theory, the language of the Setubandha may be either M. or non M. But such a vague proposition will not be of much use in the scientific study of the language in question. Hence we shall have to try other means for its proper indentification. If the language of the Setubandha is not M. it must be any one of the three dialects AMg. Mg. and Ś. containing kṣ. $>$ kh-, -kkh- which occur in the work in overwhelming number of cases as compared with kṣ. $>$ ch-, -cch- which is a M. feature. For obvious reasons the language of the Setubandha is not AMg., or Mg. and hence it may be Ś. Now this apparent rivalry between Ś. and M. to claim the Setubandha as its own is indeed a difficult problem, and this cannot be easily solved unless we are to assume a genetic connextion between the two MIA dialects Ś and M. Such a connextion was suspected by R. Hoernle long ago and the present writer too found reasons to have a similar view in this matter and the results of his investigations in this line have already been published in a paper named 'Mahārāṣṭrī, a late phase of Śaurasenī' (Journal of the Department of Letters of the Calcutta University, vol. xxxii, 1933).

In this paper we gave the following reasons in support of our view:

1. M. as a MIA. dialect came to be recognized very late (*circa* 600 A. C.).

(i) The Chapter XII of the Prākṛta-prakāśa (*c.* 600 A.C.) in which the name of M. occurs, is not from the hand of Vararuci.*

(ii) Pkt. grammarians of Western India (which is very contiguous to Mahārāṣṭra), such as Hemacandra, Śubhacandra and Śrutasāgara did not name any Pkt. as M.

(iii) Early (before 1000 A.C.) writers on poetics except Daṇḍin, did not know any M.

2. The difference between Ś. and M., which is very meagre may be explained by assuming a chronological distance between the two.

---

* In Cowell's edition the colophon of this chapter expressly ascribes it to Bhāmaha the commentator. This fact escaped my notice while writing the paper mentioned above.

भद्दं भोदु [1]सरस्सईएँ कइणो णन्दन्तु वासाइणो
अण्णाणं-पि परं पअट्टदु वरा वाणी छइल्लप्पिआ ।
[2]वच्छोमी तह मागही फुरदु णो सा किं-पि पञ्चालिआ
[3]रीदीआ ओॅलिहन्तु कव्वकुसला जोण्हं चओरा [4]विअ ॥१॥

अकलिअपरिरम्भविब्भमाइं अजाणिअचुम्बणडम्बराइँ दूरं ।
अघडिअघणताडणाइँ णिच्चं णमह अणङ्गरईण मोहणाइं ॥ २ ॥

([5]नान्द्यन्ते) सूत्रधारः ।

ससिहण्डमण्डणाणं [5]संमोहणासाण सुरअणपिआणं ।
गिरिसगिरिन्दसुआणं संघाडी वो सुहं देउ ॥ ३ ॥

अवि-अ

ईसारोसप्पसादप्पणदिसु बहुसो सग्गगङ्गाजलेणं
आमूलं पूरिदाए तुहिणकरकलारुप्पसिप्पीएँ रुद्दो ।
जोण्हामुत्ताहलिल्लं णदमउलिणिहित्तग्गहत्थेहिँ दोहिँ
अग्घं सिग्घं-व देन्तो जआदि गिरिसुआपाअपङ्करुहाणं ॥४॥

---

1. W सरस्सईए, K सरस्सईअ. 2. K वच्छोमी, W वत्थोमी, G वच्छोत्ती, N वत्थोमी. 3. ABPW रीदीआउ(=ओ) लिहन्तु, NORT रीदीओ लिहन्तु, K रीदीओ विलिहन्तु, G विलहं तु. 4. K विअ, BW इव. 5. P संमोहणासाण, NG संमोहणासाणं, BWO समोहणासाण.

(परिक्रम्य नेपथ्याभिमुखम् अवलोक्य) किं-पुण णट्टपअट्टो विअ दीसदि अम्हकुसीलवाण पवञ्चो। जदो एक्का [1]पत्तोचिआइं [2]सिचआइं उच्चिणोदि। इअरा कुसुमावलीओ गुम्फेदि। अण्णा [3]पडिसीसआइं पसारेदि। [4]कावि-हु पट्टए वण्णिआओ वट्टेदि। एस वंसो ठविदो ठाणे। इअं वीणा पडिसारीअदि। [5]इमे तिण्णि-वि मुअङ्गा सज्जीअन्ति। एस कंसतालाणं [6]पक्खालणुञ्जालणहलवोलो। एवं धुवागीदं आलवीअदि। ता किंपि [7]कुडुम्बं हक्कारिअ पुच्छिस्सं। (नेपथ्याभिमुखं संज्ञापयति)।

ततः प्रविशति

पारिपार्श्विकः। आणवेदु भाओ।

सूत्रधारः। किं-पुण णट्टपअट्टा विअ दीसध।

पारिपार्श्विकः। सट्टअं णच्चिदव्वं।

सूत्रधारः। को-उण तस्स कई।

पारिपार्श्विकः।

भाव कहिज्जदु एदं को भणइ रअणिवल्लहसिहण्डो।
रहुकुलचूडामणिणो महिन्दवालस्स को-अ गुरू॥ ५॥

---

1. AB ०चियाइं, W ०चिआइं. 2. P सिचयाइ, A सिचयाइ, W सिचियाइं. 3. G पडिसिसस्सयाइ. 4. G कावि वण्णिआ क्खु पट्टए. 5. K इमे, W एमे. 6. GDOR पक्खालणुज्जालण, W पक्खालुज्जालण, 7. BP कुडुम्बं, WI कुडम्बं G कुडुम्बअ, O कुडुम्बादी.

सूत्रधारः । (विचिन्त्य) अए पण्होत्तरं एदं । (प्रकाशं) राअसेहरो ।

पारिपार्श्विकः । सो एदस्स कई ।

सूत्रधारः । (स्मृत्वा) कथिदं [1]जेव छइल्लेहिं ।

सो सट्टओ-त्ति भण्णइ दूरं जो [2]णाडिआएँ अणुहरदि ।
किं-पुण पवेसअविक्खम्भआइ इह केवलं णत्थि ॥ ६ ॥

विचिन्त्य । ता किं-ति[3] सक्कअं परिहरिअ पाईअवन्धे पअट्टो कई[4] ।

पारिपार्श्विकः । [5]सव्वभासा-चदुरेण तेण भणिदं [6]जेव [7]जहा

अत्थविसेसा ते च्चिअ सद्दा [8]ते च्चेव परिणमन्ता-वि ।
उत्तिविसेसो कव्वं भासा जा होउ सा होउ ॥ ७ ॥

सूत्रधारः । ता अप्पा किं ण वण्णिदो तेण ।

पारिपार्श्विकः । सुणदु । वण्णिदो जेव तक्कालकईणं मज्झम्मि मअङ्कलेहाकहाकारेण अवराइएण, [9]जधा

बालकई कइराओ णिब्भरराअस्स तह उवज्झाओ ।
[10]इअ जस्स पएहिँ परम्पराएँ माहप्पमारूढं ॥ ८ ॥
सोँ एअस्स कई सिरिराअसेहरो तिहुअणं-पि धवलेन्ति ।
हरिणङ्कपाडिसिद्धीएँ णिक्कलङ्का गुणा जस्स ॥ ९ ॥

---

1. R ज्जेव, B ज्जेव, W चेव. 2. W णाडिआए, P ०डिआइ. 3. K ति, W त्ति. 4. *See* Notes. 5. K चदुरेण W चतुरेण. 6. R ज्जेव, B ज्जेव, W चेव. 7. K जधा, W जहा. 8. B तच्चेव, W त्तिचेव. 9. K जधा, W *om.* 10. G इदि अजस्स परम्पराए जघा.

सूत्रधारः । ता केण [1]समादिट्ठा पउञ्जध ।

पारिपार्श्विकः ।

चाहुआणकुलमउलिमालिआ राअसेहरकइन्दगेहिणी ।
भत्तुणो किदिमवन्तिसुन्दरी सा पउञ्जइदुमेदमिच्छदि[2] ॥१०॥

किं-च

चण्डवालधरणीहरिणङ्को चक्कवट्टिपअलाहणिमित्तं ।
एत्थ सट्टअवरे रससोत्ते कुन्तलाहिवसुदं परिणेदि ॥ ११ ॥

ता भाव एहि । अणन्तरकरणिज्जं [3]संपाडेम्ह । जदो [4]महाराअस्स [5]देईए भूमिअं घेत्तूण [6]अज्जा अज्जभारिआ-अ जवणिअन्तरे [7]चिट्ठदि । (इति परिक्रम्य निष्क्रान्तौ) ।

प्रस्तावना ।

ततः प्रविशति राजा देवी विदूषको विभवतश्च परिवारः । सर्वे परिक्रम्य यथोचितम् उपविशन्ति ।

राजा । देवि दक्खिणाहिवणरिन्दणन्दणे[8] वद्धावीआसि वसन्तारम्भेण । जदो

बिम्बोट्ठे बहलं ण देन्ति मअणं णो गन्धतेलाइरा
वेणीओ विरअन्ति लेन्ति ण तहा अङ्गम्मि कुप्पासअं ।

---

1. K °दिट्ठा, W °इट्ठा. 2. K °दि, W °ति. 3. W संपाडम्ह, K संपादि-. 4. N °राअस्स, W °राअ°. 5. N देईए, W Wदेवीए. 6. P आज्जा, K अज्जो. 7. G चिट्ठदि, W चिट्ठंति, PN वट्टदि. 8. OW °न्दणी, K °ण्डिणि.

जं बाला मुहकुङ्कुमम्मि-वि[1] घणे वट्टन्ति ढिल्लाअरा
तं मण्णे सिसिरं विणिज्जिअ बला पत्तो [2]वसन्तूसवो ॥१२॥

देवी। अहं-पि पडिवद्धाविआ भविस्सं। जधा

[3]छोल्लन्ति दन्तरअणाइ गदे तुसारे
ईसीसि चन्दणरसम्मि मणं कुणन्ति।
एण्हिं सुवन्ति घरमज्झिमसालिआसु
[4]पाअन्तपुञ्जिदपडं मिहुणाइँ पेच्छ ॥ १३ ॥

(नेपथ्ये) वैतालिकयोरेकः। जअ पुव्वदिगङ्गणाभुअङ्ग चम्पाचम्पअकण्णऊर राढाजणिदराढ चङ्गत्तणणिज्जिदकामरूव हरिकेलीकेलिआर [5]अवमण्णिअकण्णसुवण्णदाण सव्वङ्गसुन्दरत्तणरमणिज्ज सुहाअ देवस्स भोदु सुरहिसमअसमारम्भो। इह हि

पण्डीणं गण्डवालीपुलअणचवला कञ्चिबालाबलाणं
माणं दोखण्डअन्ता रदिरहसअरा चोडचोडालआणं।
कण्णाडीणं कुणन्ता कुरलतरलणं कुन्तलीणं पिएसुं
गुम्फन्ता गेहगण्ठिं मलअसिहरिणो सिंघला एन्ति वाआ ॥

(अत्रैव) द्वितीयः।

जादं कुङ्कुमपङ्कलीढरमणीगण्डप्पहं चम्पअं
थोआवट्टिददुद्धमुद्धकुसुमा पप्फुल्लिआ मल्लिआ।
मूले सामलमग्गलग्गभसलं लक्खिज्जए किंसुअं
पिज्जन्तं भमरेहिँ दोहि-वि दिसाभाएसु लग्गेहि-व ॥१५

1. K वि, W व. 2. K वसन्तूसवो, W वसन्तोसवो. 3. K छोल्लन्ति, W छोल्लंति. 4. BOA ॰पुञ्जिद॰, W ॰पुञ्जित. 5. STU ॰मण्णिदकण्ण-(U॰ण्ण)सुवण्णदाण, K ॰मण्णिदअण्णसुवण्णदाण.

राजा। पिए विब्भमलेहे को अहं [1]वद्धावओ तुज्झ का तुमं-पि वद्धाविआ मज्झ। किं-पुण दो-वि अम्हे वद्धाविआ कञ्चणचण्डरअणचण्डेहिं वन्दीहिं। ता [2]विब्भमपअट्टावअं [3]तरट्टीणं णट्टावअं मलअमारुदन्दोलिदचन्दणलदाणच्चणीणं[4] चारुपवञ्चिदपञ्चमं [5]कलकण्ठिकण्ठेसु कन्दलिदकन्दप्पकोदण्डदण्डचण्डिमं णिद्धवन्धवं वसुन्धरापुरन्धीए ता वित्थारिदपसइप्पमाणच्छिणी महोच्छवं जहिच्छं पेच्छ।

देवी। [6]जधा णिवेदिदं वन्दीहिं पअट्टा ज्जेव मलआणिला। [7]तधा-अ

लङ्कातोरणमालिआतरलिणो [8]कुम्भुब्भवस्सासमे
मन्दन्दोलिदचन्दणद्दुमलदा कप्पूरसम्पक्किणो।
कङ्कोलीकुलकम्पिणो फणिलदाणिप्पट्टणट्टावआ
चण्डं चुम्बिदतम्बपण्णिसलिला वाअन्ति चेत्ताणिला ॥१६॥

अवि-अ

माणं [9]मुञ्चध देह वल्लहजणे दिट्ठं तरङ्गुत्तरं
तारुण्णं दिअहाइँ पञ्च दह वा पीणत्थणुत्थम्भणं।
[10]इत्थं कोइलमञ्जुसिञ्जिदमिसा देवस्स पञ्चेसुणो
दिण्णा चेत्तमहूसवेण सहसा आण-व्व सव्वङ्कसा ॥१७॥

---

1. W वद्धावउ. 2. K विब्भमप्पअट्टा°. W विब्भममरट्टपअट्टा°. 3. K तरट्टीणं. W तरुडीणं. 4. K णच्चणीणं, W णच्चईणीणं. 5. K कलकण्ठी°, W कलअण्ठी°. 6. K जधा, AWOD जहा. 7. K तधा, WBOD तहा. 8. K कुम्भुब्भ°, B कुंभअभ°, W कुंभीभ°. 9. BNOR मुञ्चध, WPA मुञ्चद. 10. K इत्थं, W इत्थी.

विदूषकः । भो तुम्हाणं [1]सव्वस्सिं मज्झे अहं [2]एक्को कालक्खरिओ जस्स मे ससुरओ[3] परघरेसु पोत्थाइ वहन्तओ आसि ।

चेटी । (विहस्य) तदो कमागदं ते पण्डिच्चं ।

विदूषकः । (सक्रोधम्) आ दासीए धूदे भविस्सकुट्टिणि णिल्लक्खणे अविअक्खणे ईदिसोहं मुक्खो जं तए-वि[4] उवहसीआमि । अण्णं-च रे परपुत्तविट्टालिणि भमरटेण्टे टेण्टाकराले तुट्टिसंघट्टिदे—अह वा हत्थे कङ्कणं किं दप्पणेण ।

विचक्षणा । एवं णेदं । तुरङ्गस्स सिग्घत्तणे किं सक्खिणो पुच्छिअन्ति । ता वण्णअ वसन्तं ।

विदूषकः । कधं [5]पञ्जरगदा सारि-व्व कुरुकुरुअन्ती चिट्ठसि । ण किं-पि जाणासि । ता [6]पिअवअस्सस्स देवीए पुरदो पढिस्सं । जदो ण कत्थूरिआ गामे वणे वा [7]विक्किणीअदि । णेदं सुवण्णं जं कसवट्टिअं विणा कसीअदि । (इति पठति)

फुल्लुक्करं कलमकूरसमं वहन्ति
जे सिन्धुवारविडवा मह वल्लहा ते ।
जे गालिअस्स महिसीदहिणो सरिच्छा
ते किं-च मुद्धविअइल्लपसूणपुञ्जा ॥ १८ ॥

विचक्षणा । (विहस्य) णिअकन्तारत्तणजोग्गं ते[8] वअणं ।

---

1. W सव्वेसिं. 2. K एक्को, WPB एकी. 3. W ससुरउ. 4. K वि, WT *om.* वि. 5. K पञ्जरगदा, W दंजरगभा. 6. NRSV पिअवअस्सस्स देवीए, K पिअवअस्सदेवीणं. 7. K विक्किणीअदि, W विक्कणीयदि. 8. K तै, W दे.

विदूषकः । किं-पि उदारवअणा [1]तुमं पढ ।

देवी । (किञ्चित् स्मित्वा) सहि विअक्खणे अम्हाणं पुरदो तुवं गाढकइअत्तणेण उत्ताणा भोसि । ता पढ सम्पदं अज्जउत्तस्स पुरदो सअं-कदं कव्वं । जदो तं कव्वं जं सभाए पढीअदि । तं सुवण्णं जं कसवट्टिआए णिव्वहदि । सा घरिणी जा पदिं रञ्जेदि ।

विचक्षणा । जं देवी आणवेदि । (इति पठति)

जे [2]लङ्कागिरिमेहलाहिँ खलिदा सम्भोअखिण्णोरई-
 फारप्फुल्लफणावलीकवलणे पत्ता दरिद्दत्तणं ।
ते एण्हिं मलआणिला विरहिणीणीसाससम्पक्किणो
 जादा झत्ति सिसुत्तणे-वि बहला तारुण्णपुण्णा विअ ॥१९॥

राजा । सच्चं विअक्खणा विअक्खणा [3]चदुरत्तणे [4]उत्तीणं । [5]ता किं-पि अण्णं विचित्तदाए[6] । कईणं सुकइ-त्ति । कविचूडामणित्तणे ठिदा एसा ।

विदूषकः । (सक्रोधम्) ता उज्जुअं [7]जेव किं ण भणइ अच्चुत्तमा विअक्खणा [8]अच्चाधमो कविञ्जलो बम्भणो-त्ति ।

विचक्षणा । अज्ज मा कुप्प । कव्वं जेव कवित्तणं पिसुणेदि । जदो णिअकन्तारत्तणणिन्दणिज्जे वि अत्थे सुकुमारा

1. K तुमं, W तुमंपि. 2. W ०मेखलाहिं. 3. NG चदुरत्तणे, W चडुरत्तणे. 4. K उत्तीणं, W चदुरत्तीर्णा. 5. 5 B ता किंपि अण्णं विचित्तादाए, W ता अ किमण्णं चदुरत्तणविचित्तदाए. 6. *See* Notes. 7. A ज्जेव, B दोव, W ख्खेव(?). 8. B अच्चाधमो, W अच्चाधम्मं.

[1]वाणी लम्बत्थणीए विअ एक्कावली [2]तुण्डिलाए विअ कञ्चुलिआ काणाए विअ कज्जलसलाआ सुदट्ठुदरं ण भादि रमणिज्जा ।

विदूषकः । [3]तुब्भ उण रमणिज्जे-वि अत्थे ण सुन्दरा सद्दावली । कणअकडिसुत्तए विअ [4]लोहकिङ्कणीमालिआ पडिपट्टे विअ टसरिविरअणा गोरङ्गीए [5]विअ चन्दणचच्चा ण चारुत्तणं अवलम्बेदि । तधा-वि तुवं[6] वण्णिआसि ।

विचक्षणा । अज्ज का तुम्हेहि समं [7]अम्हाणं पाडिसिद्धी । जदो तुवं णाराओ विअ णिरक्खरो-वि [8]रअणतुलाए णिउज्जीअसि । अहं पुण तुल-व्व लद्धक्खरा-वि ण [9]सुवण्णतोलणे णिउज्जीआमि ।

विदूषकः । (सक्रोधम्) एवं मह भणन्तीए तुह दक्खिणं-च [10]जुहिट्ठिलजेट्ठभाअरणामधेअं अङ्गं [11]तडत्ति [12]उप्पाडइस्सं ।

विचक्षणा । तुज्झ पुणो-हं उत्तरफग्गुणीपुरस्सरणामधेअं अङ्गं [13]तडत्ति खण्डिस्सं ।

राजा । वअस्स [14]कइत्तणे [15]ठिदा एसा ।

विदूषकः । (सक्रोधम्) ता उज्जुअं ज्जेव किं ण [16]भणइ

---

1. K *has* इ *before* वाणी. 2. W तुंडिल्लाए, K तुन्दिल्लाए. 3. W तुब्भ, K तुज्भ. 4. WN °किंकणी°. 5. K विश्व, W विव. 6. B तुवं, K तुमं. 7. K *om.* अम्हाणं *after* समं. 8. K °तुलाए, W °तुल्लाए. 9. K सुवण्णतोलणे, WPR सुअण्णत्ते वि. 10. W जुहिट्ठिल, K जुहिट्ठिर. 11. K तडत्ति, B तडित्त. 12. K उप्पाडइस्सं, W उप्पाडयस्सं. 13. K तडत्ति, B तडित्त. 14. K कइत्तणे, W कयत्तणे. 15. K ठिदा, W णिठिदा. 16. K भणइ, W भणेइ.

अम्हाणं चेडिआ [1]हरिडड्ढ-णन्दिउड्ढ-पोट्टिस-हालप्पहुदीणं-पि पुरदो सुकइ-त्ति । (परिक्रामति)

राजा । एवं [2]णेदं ।

विदूषकः रुष्ट इव सक्रोधम् उत्थाय परिक्रामति ।

विचक्षणा । (विहस्य) तहिं गच्छ जहिं मे मादाए पढम-[3]साडोलिआ गदा ।

विदूषकः । (वलितग्रीवम्) तुवं पुण तहिं गच्छ जहिं मे मादाए पढमा दन्तावली गदा । [4]अण्णं च ईदिसस्स राउलस्स भद्दं भोदु जहिं चेडिआ [5]बम्भणेण समं समसीसिआए दीसादि, मइरा पञ्चगव्वं-च [6]एक्कस्सिं भण्डे कीरादि । कच्चं माणिक्कं च समं आहरणे पउञ्जीअदि ।

विचक्षणा । इह राउले[7] तं ते[8] भोदु कण्ठट्ठिदं जं तिलोअणो भअवं[9] सीसे समुव्वहदि । तेणं च दे मुहं चूरीअदु जेण असोअतरू[10] दोहलं लहेदि ।

विदूषकः । आ दासीए पुत्ति. टेण्टाकराले कोससअचट्टणि[11] रच्छालोट्टणि एवं मं भणसि । ता मह महबम्भणस्स भणिदेण तं तुमं लह[12] जं फग्गुणसमए सोहञ्जणो [13]जणादो लहेदि जं-च

1. K हरिड्ढ etc., W हरियड्डणंदियड्डपुट्टिस०. 2. W नेदं. 3. W साडोलिआ, BP साडुल्लिआ (या). 4. W अन्नं च. 5. W बंभणेण, K बम्हणेण. 6. K एक्कस्सिं भण्डए, W एगम्मि भंडे. 7. W राउले, K राअउले. 8. AN ते, K दे, W om. 9. WOB भअ' *after* तिलोअणो, K *before* तिलो०. 10. W *add.* तरुणीणं. 11. W कोससयच, P कोसासय, N कोससअल. 12. K लह, W लहह. 13. WRT जणादो, K दोहलो *for* जणादो, BPO *om.*

पामराहिं-तो [1]गलिबइल्लो लहेदि ।

विचक्षणा । अहं पुण [2]तुह एवं भणन्तस्स [3]णेउरस्स विअ पाअ-लग्गस्स पाएण मुहं चूरइस्सं[4] । अण्णं च [5]उत्तरासाढापुरस्सर-णक्खत्तणामधेअं अङ्गजुअलं उप्पाडिअ घलिस्सं ।

विदूषकः सक्रोधं परिक्रामति ।

(जवनिकान्तरे किञ्चिदुच्चैः[6]) [7]ईदिसं राउलं दूरेण वन्दीअदि जहिं दासी बम्भणेण समं पडिसिद्धीं करेदि । ता अज्जप्पहुदि णिअवसुन्धराणामबम्भणीए चलणसुस्सूसओ[8] भविअ गेहे ज्जेव चिट्ठिस्सं ।

सव्वे हसन्ति ।

देवी । कीदिसी अज्ज-कविञ्जलेण विणा गोट्ठी कीदिसी उण णअणञ्जणेण विणा पसाहणालच्छी ।

(नेपथ्ये [विदूषकः])

ण-हु ण-हु आगमिस्सं । अण्णो को-वि पिअवअस्सो वअस्सेण अण्णेसीअदु । एसा वा[9] दुट्ठदासी लम्बकुच्चं टप्परकण्णं पडिसीसअं देइअ मह ठाणे कीरदु[10] । अहं एक्को मुदो तुम्हाणं सव्वाणं मज्झम्मि[11] । तुम्हे उण वरिससअं जीवध ।

---

1. K गलिवइल्ल, W गलियवयलो. 2. W तुम्ह *for* तुह. 3. W णेवरस्स *for* णेउरस्स. 4. W चुरिइस्सं. 5. WN ०साढ०. 6. *See* Note. 7. W इदिस्सं. 8. K सुस्सूसओ, W ०सगो. 9. K वा, W *om.* 10. APWNR कीरदु, K करीअदु. 11. PW मज्झम्मि, K मज्झे.

राजा । [1]कविञ्जलेण विणा कुदो हिअअस्स णिव्वुदि[2] ।

विचक्षणा । मा अणुसन्धेध । अणुणअकक्कसो [3]खु कविञ्जलओ [4]बम्भणो सलिलसित्तो[5] सणगुणगण्ठी दिढं गाढअरो भोदि[6] ।

देवी । (समन्तादवलोक्य)

गाअन्तगोवअवहूपअपेंखिदासु
दोलासु विब्भमवदीसु णिविट्ठदिट्ठी ।
जं जादि [7]खञ्जिदतुरङ्गरहो दिणेसो
तेण-व्व होन्ति दिअहा अइदीहदीहा ॥ २० ॥

प्रविश्य पटाक्षेपेण

विदूषकः । आसणं आसणं ।

राजा । किं तेण ।

विदूषकः । [8]भइरवाणन्दो दुवारे । उवविस्सदि[9] ।

राजा । किं सो जो जणवअणादो [10]अच्चब्भुदसिद्धी सुणीआदि ।

विदूषकः । अध किं ।

राजा । पवेसअ ।

विदूषको निष्क्रम्य तेनैव सह प्रविशति ।

1. APWO *have this sentence.* 2. W निव्वुदी. 3. APW खु, K क्खु. 4. PBWO *om.* बम्हणो. 5. K *add* विष. 6. W होदि. 7. W खंचिद, PPORU खंजिद, K खंजिष. 8. *See* Note. 9. W उववियदि, B उपविस्सदि, P उपविसदि, A उपवेस्सदि, K चिट्ठदि. 10. K अच्चब्भुद०, W अच्चब्भुअ०.

भैरवानन्दः। (किञ्चिन् मदम् अभिनीय)

[1]मन्तो ण तन्तो ण-अ किं-पि जाणे[2]
[3]झाणं-च ण किं-पि गुरुप्पसादा।
मज्जं पिवामो महिलं रमामो
मोक्खं-च जामो कुलमग्गलग्गा ॥ २१ ॥

अवि-अ

रण्डा चण्डा दिक्खिदा[4] धम्मदारा
मज्जं मंसं पिज्जए खज्जए-अ।
भिक्खा भोज्जं चम्मखण्डं-च सेज्जा
कोलो धम्मो कस्स णो भादि रम्मो ॥ २२ ॥

किं-च

मुत्तिं भणन्ति हरिबम्हमुहा-वि देवा
झाणेण वेअपढणेण कदुक्किआहिं।
एक्केण केवलमुमादइदेण दिट्ठो
मोक्खो समं सुरअकेलिसुरारसेहिं ॥ २३ ॥

राजा। इदं आसणं। उवविसदु भइरवाणन्दो।

भैरवानन्दः। (उपविश्य) किं कादव्वं।

राजा। कहिं-पि विसए अच्छरिअं दट्ठूं इच्छामि।

1. ABPWO मंतो ण तंतो ण अ किं पि, K मन्ताण तन्ताण ण किं पि. 2. K जाणे, W झाणं. 3. K झाणं, W जाणं. 4. APNR दिक्खिदा, W दिक्खदा, B सिक्खिदा.

भैरवानन्दः ।

दंसेमि तं-पि ससिणं [1]वसुहावइण्णं
थम्भेमि तस्स-वि रविस्स रहं णहद्धे ।
आणेमि [2]जक्खसुरसिद्धगणङ्गणाओ
तं णत्थि भूमिवलए मह जं ण सज्झं ॥२४॥

ता भण किं कीरदु ।

राजा । वअस्स भण किं-पि अउव्वं दिट्ठं महिलारअणं ।

विदूषकः । अत्थि एत्थ दक्खिणावहे [3]वच्छोमं णाम णअरं । तहिं मए एक्कं [4]कण्णआरअणं दिट्ठं । तं इह आणीअदु ।

भैरवानन्दः । आणीअदि ।

राजा । अवदारिज्जदु पुण्णिमाहरिणङ्को [5]धरणीअलम्मि ।

भैरवानन्दो ध्यानं नाटयति ।

ततः प्रविशति पटाक्षेपेण नायिका । सर्व्वेऽवलोकयन्ति ।

राजा । अहह अच्छरिअं अच्छरिअं ।

जं धोअञ्जणसोणलोअणजुअं लग्गालअग्गं मुहं
हत्थालम्बिदकेसपल्लवचए दोलन्ति जं बिन्दुणो ।
जं एक्कं सिचअञ्चलं णिवसिदं तं ण्हाणकेलिट्ठिदा
आणीदा [6]इअमब्भूदेक्कजणणी जोईसरेणामुणा ॥२५॥

---

1. W ०वद्दन्नं. 2. W जक्खु०. 3. K वच्छोमं, W वत्थोवरं. 4. K कण्णा०, W कण्णाया०. 5. APW धरणीयलम्मि, B ०णीयले. 6. W ०मब्भुदिक्क, ABNORTU ०मब्भुदेक्क, K ०मब्भुएक्क०.

अवि-अ

एक्केण पाणिणलिणेण णिवेसअन्ती
वत्थञ्चलं घणथणत्थलसंसमाणं ।
चित्ते लिहिज्जदि ण कस्स-वि संजमन्ती
अण्णेण [1]चङ्कमणदो चलिदं कडिल्लं ॥ २६ ॥

विदूषकः ।

ण्हाणावमुक्काहरणुच्चआए तरङ्गभङ्गक्खदमण्डणाए ।
[2]ओल्लंसुउल्लासिथणुल्लआए सुन्देरसव्वस्समिमीएँ दिट्ठी ॥२७॥

नायिका । (सर्व्वानवलोक्य स्वगतम्) एस महाराओ को-वि इमिणा गम्भीरमहुरेण सोहासमुदएण जाणीअदि । एसा-वि एदस्स महादेवी [3]लक्खीअदि । अद्धणारीस्सरस्स वामद्धे अकहिआ-वि[4] गोरी [5]मुणीज्जदि । एसो-वि जोईसरो । एस उण परिअणो । (विचिन्त्य) ता किं-ति एदस्स महिला-सहिदस्स-वि दिट्ठी मं बहु मण्णेदि । (इति त्र्यस्रं वीक्षते)

राजा । (विदूषकमपवार्य्य)

जं मुक्का सवणन्तरेण सहसा तिक्खा कडक्खच्छडा
[6]भिङ्गाहिट्ठिदकेदअ-अग्गिमदलद्दोणीसरिच्छच्छवी ।
तं कप्पूररसेण णं धवलिदो जोह्लाएँ णं ण्हाविदो
मुत्ताणं घणरेणुण-व्व छुरिदो जादो-म्हि एत्थन्तरे ॥ २८ ॥

---

1. ANORSTU मणदो, W ०मणिदो. 2. W ०थणुल्लदाए, B
3. W लच्चीअदि, O लक्खीअदि, O मुणीज्जदि. 4. K वि, W इ. 5. WP सुणिज्जदि. 6. W भिंगाहिट्ठिद०, P भिंगाहिट्ठिद०. 7. K ०सरिच्छ०, W ०सरिसस०.

(विदूषकं तथैव)। अहो से [1]रूवसोहा।

मण्णे मज्झं तिवलिवलिअं [2]डिम्भमुट्ठिऍ गेज्झं
णो बाहुहिं रमणफलअं वेडिदुं जादि दोहिं।
णेत्तच्छेत्तं तरुणपसईकिज्जमाणोवमाणं
ता पच्चक्खं [3]मह विलिहिदुं जादि एसा ण चित्ते ॥२९॥

[4]कहं ण्हाणधोदविलेवणा-वि समुत्तारिदभूसणा-वि रमणिज्जा। अह-वा

रूवेण [5]मुक्काओ˘ [6]विभूसीअन्ति ताणं अलंकारवसेण सोहा।
णिसग्गचङ्गस्स ण[7] माणुसस्स सोहा समुम्मीलदि भूसणेहिं ॥३०

एदाए एदं दाव। जदो

लावण्णं णवजच्चकञ्चणणिहं णेत्ताण दीहत्तणं
कण्णेहिं खलिदं कवोलफलआ [8]दोखण्डचन्दोवमा।
एसा पञ्चसरेण सन्धिदधणुद्दण्डेण रक्खिज्जए
जेणं सोसणमोहणप्पहुदिणो विन्धन्ति मं मग्गणा ॥३१॥

विदूषकः। (विहस्य) [9]जाणे रच्छासु लुण्ठदि तुह सोण्डरित्तणं।

राजा। (विहस्य) पिअवअस्स कधेमि दे।

अङ्गं चङ्गं णिअगुणगणालंकिदं कामिणीणं
पच्छाअन्ती तणुगुणसिरिं भादि णेवच्छलच्छी।

---

1. WNOR रूअ०. 2. W ०मुट्ठइ. 3. K मह, W महि.
4. *See* Notes *on this.* 5. B मुकाउ, A मुत्ताओ, K मुक्का वि.
6. PRSTU विभू०, W विहुसीअन्ति. 7. STU व. 8. K दोखण्ड,
AWO दोहंड. 9. A जाणिमि रथ्यासु लुंठदि तुह सोंडीरत्तणं, W जाणीदि
ज्जेव रच्छाकाए से लुट्ठिज्जइ सोडी०, K जाणादि रच्छावादो लुब्बी सोंडीरत्तणं.

इत्थं जाणं अवअवगदा का-वि सुन्देरमुद्दा
मण्णे ताणं [1]वलइदधणू णिच्चभिच्चो अणङ्गो ॥ ३२ ॥

[2]अवि-अ एदाए

तहा रमणवित्थरो जह ण ठादि कञ्चीलदा
तहा [3]सिहिणतुङ्गिमा जह णिएइ णाहि ण-हु ।
तहा णअणवड्ढिमा जह ण किं-पि कण्णुप्पलं
तहा-अ मुहमुज्जलं दुससिणी जहा पुण्णिमा ॥३३॥

देवी । अज्ज कविञ्जल पुच्छिअ जाण का एस-त्ति ।

विदूषकः । (तां प्रति) एहि मुद्धमुहि [4]उवविसिअ णिवेदेहि का तुमं-ति ।

देवी । आसणं इमीए ।

विदूषकः । एदं मे उत्तरीअं ।

विदूषकनायिके वस्त्रदानेन उपवेशने नाटयतः[5] ।

विदूषकः । सम्पदं कहिज्जदु ।

नायिका । अत्थि एत्थ [7]दक्खिणावहे कुन्तलेसुं सअलजणवल्लहो वल्लहराओ णाम राआ ।

देवी । (स्वगतम्) जो मह माउच्छओ होदि[8] ।

नायिका । तस्स घरणी ससिप्पहा णाम ।

देवी । सा-वि मे माउच्छिआ ।

---

1. ANR वलइद०, W वलइव०. 2. K अवि-अ, W अन्नं च. 3. W सिहण०. 4. WU उपविसिअ. 5. W *add.* नायका उपविशति. 6. W *add.* का तुमं ति. 7. W ०वहे, B पहे, K ०वघे. 8. K भोदि PNWOR होइ.

नायिका । (विहस्य) तेहिं अहं [1]खलखण्डेहिं कीदा दुहिद-त्ति वुच्चामि ।

देवी । (स्वगतम्) ण हि [2]ससिप्पहागब्भं अन्तरेण ईदिसी [3]रूवसोहा । णो वा [4]विदूरभूमिगब्भुप्पत्तिं अन्तरेण वेरुलिअमणिसलाआ णिप्पज्जन्ति । (प्रकाशं) णं तुवं कप्पूरमञ्जरी ।

नायिका [5]अधोमुखी तिष्ठति ।

[6]देवी । एहि बहिणिए आलिङ्गसु मं (इति परिष्वजेते) ।

नायिका । अम्ह-कप्पूरमञ्जरीए [7]एसो पढमपणामो ।

देवी । अज्ज मए भइरवाणन्द तुज्झ पसाएण [8]अपूव्वं संविहाणअं अणुभविदं बहिणिआए दंसणेण । चिट्ठदु दाव [9]पञ्चसत्तदिवसाइं । पच्छा झाणविमाणेण पुणो णइस्सध ।

भैरवानन्दः । जं भणदि देवी ।

विदूषकः । (राजानम् उद्दिश्य) अम्हे परं इत्थ दुवे-वि बाहिरा तुवं अहं च । जदो एदाणं मिलिदं [10]कुडुम्बं वट्टदि । [11]जदो इमीओ दो-वि बहिणिआओ । भइरवाणन्दो उण एदाणं सञ्जोअअरो अग्घिदो महग्घिदो । एसा विअक्खणा महीअलसरस्सई कुट्टिणी-देवी ज्जेव देहन्तरेण वट्टदि ।

---

1. K खलखण्डेहिं, W खलक्खंडेण. 2. W ०गब्भमन्तरेण. 3. K रूव०, W रूम०. 4. W ०गब्भुप्पत्तिमन्तरेण. 5. K अ० तिष्ठति, W अहोमुही चिट्ठदि. 6. W *om.* देवी. 7. W एसो *before* कप्पू०. 8. K अपूव्वं, W अउव्वं. 9. K दिवसाइं, WO दिवहाइं. 10. K कुडुम्बं, W कुडम्बं. 11. W *om.* जदो.

देवी । विअक्खणे [1]णिअजेट्ठबहिणिअं सुलक्खणं [2]भणिअ भइरवाणन्दस्स हिअइच्छिदा सपज्जा कादव्वा ।

विचक्षणा । जं देवी आणवेदि[3] ।

[4]देवी । (राजानं प्रति) अज्जउत्त पेसेहि मं जेण बहिणीए एदावत्थाए णेवच्छलच्छीलीलाणिमित्तं अन्तेउरं गमिस्सं ।

राजा । जुज्जदि चम्पअलदाए [5]कत्थूरिआकप्पूररसेहिं आलवालपूरणं ।

(नेपथ्ये) वैतालिकयोरेकः । सुहसञ्झा भोदु देवस्स ।

एदं [6]वासरजीवपिण्डंसरिसं चण्डंसुणो मण्डलं
को जाणादि कहिं-पि सम्पदि गदं पत्तम्मि कालन्तरे ।
जादा किं-च इअं-पि दीहविरहा सोऊण[5] णाहे गदे
णिद्दामुद्दिदलोअण-व्व णलिणी मीलन्तपङ्केरुहा ॥३४॥

द्वितीयः[6] ।

उग्घाडिज्जन्ती [7]लीलामणिमअवलहीचित्तभित्तिणिवेसा
पलङ्का किङ्करीहिं [8]उदुसमअसुहा पत्थरिज्जन्ति झत्ति ।
सेरन्धीलोलहत्थङ्गुलिचलणवसा [9]पट्टसद्दो पअट्टो
हुंकारो मण्डवेसु विलसदि महुरो रुद्दतुट्ठङ्गणाणं ॥३५॥

राजा । अम्हे-वि सञ्झं वन्दिदुं गमिस्सामो ।

इति निष्क्रान्ताः सर्वे ।

प्रथमं जवनिकान्तरम् ।

---

1. W ०वहिणिय०. 2. K भणिअ, W भणीय. 3. W *add.* तं कुणंमि. 4. W *om.* देवी. 5. W सोउण, K सोऊण. 6. W *add.* पठति. 7. W ०चित्ति० *for* ०चित्त०. 8. W उडु० *for* उदु०. 9. W ०सद्दो० *for* सद्दो.

ततः प्रविशति राजा प्रतीहारी च ।

(परिक्रामितकेन) प्रतीहारी । इदो इदो महाराओ ।

राजा । (कतिचित् पदानि दत्वा ताम् अनुसन्धाय)

तहिं खु अवसरे

णो[1] ठाणाहिं तिलन्तरं-पि चलिदा सुत्था णिअम्बत्थली
[2]थोउव्वेल्लवलीतरङ्गमुदरं कण्ठो [3]तिरिच्छिट्ठिदो ।
वेणीए उण आणणेन्दुभमणे लद्धं थणालिङ्गणं
जादा तीए चउव्विहा तणुलदा तंसं वलन्ती मए ॥१॥

प्रतीहारी । (स्वगतम्) कहं अज्ज-वि सो च्चेव [3]सिरिताडीसञ्चओ ताओ च्चेव अक्खरपंतीओ । ता वसन्तवण्णणेण सिढिल-आमि से तग्गदं [4]हिदआवज्जं । (प्रकाशं) [5]दिट्ठिं देदु महाराओ ईसीसि जरढाअमाणे कुसुमाअरम्मि ।

मूलाहिं-तो परहुदवहूकण्ठमुद्दं दलन्ता
देन्ता दीहमहुरिमगुणं जम्पिए छप्पआणं ।
संचारेन्ता विरहिसु णवं पञ्चमं किं-च राअं
राउम्मत्ता रइकुलहरा वासरा वित्थरन्ति ॥ २ ॥

राजा । (तद् अनाकर्ण्य सानुरागं)

आत्थाणीजणलोअणाण बहला लावण्णकल्लोलिणी
लीलाविब्भमहासवासणअरी [6]सोहग्गपालित्तिआ ।

---

1. K ण, W णो. 2. K थोउव्वेल्ल०, W थोउव्विल्ल०. 3. K तिरिच्छि०, W तिरित्थो०. 3. K ०संचओ, W ०संचउ०. 4. K हिदआवज्ज, W माणसं. 5. K देदु, CWNORS देउ. 6. K ०पालित्तिआ, W ०पालिङ्ढिआ.

णेत्तेन्दीवरदीहिआ मह पुणो सिङ्गारसञ्जीविणी
जं जादा अह मम्महेण धणुहे तिक्खो सरो सन्धिदो ॥३॥

(सोन्मादमिव) दंसणक्खणादो पहुदि कुरङ्गच्छीए

चित्ते [1]वहुट्टदि ण [2]खुट्टादि सा गुणेसुं
सेज्जाएँ लुट्टदि विसट्टदि दिङ्मुहेसुं ।
वोलम्मि वट्टदि पअट्टदि कव्वबन्धे
झाणे ण तुट्टदि चिरं तरुणी [3]तरट्टी ॥ ४ ॥

[4]अवि-अ

जे [5]तीएँ तिक्खचलचक्खुतिहाअदिट्ठा
ते कामचन्दमहुपञ्चममारणिज्जा ।
जेसुं पुणो णिवडिदा सअला-वि दिट्ठी
वट्टन्ति ते तिलञ्जलिदाणजोग्गा ॥ ५ ॥

(संस्मरणमिव) अवि-अ

अग्गम्मि भिङ्गसरणी णअणाण तीए
मज्झे पुणो कढिददुद्धतरङ्गमाला ।
पच्छा-अ से सरदि तंसणिरिक्खिदेसुं
आअण्णमण्डलिदचावहरो अणङ्गो ॥ ६ ॥

(विचिन्त्य) चिराअदि वअस्सो ।

---

1. W चहुट्टदि. 2. K खुट्टदि, W हुट्टदि. 3. K तरट्टी W तरच्छी. 4. W *om.* 5. W तीइ.

प्रविश्य विदूषको विचक्षणा च परिक्रामतः ।

विदूषकः । [1]अइ विअक्खणे सव्वं सच्चं एदं[2] ।

विचक्षणा । सव्वं सच्चअरं ।

विदूषकः । णाहं पत्तिआमि जदो परिहाससीला खु तुवं ।

विचक्षणा । अज्ज मा एवं भण । अण्णो वक्करकालो अण्णो कज्जावआरकालो ।

विदूषकः । (पुरो विलोक्य) एसो पिअवअस्सो हंसो विअ मुक्कमाणसो करी विअ [3]मअक्खामो मुणालदंण्डो विअ घणघम्ममिलाणो दिणदिण्णदीवो विअ विअलिअच्छाओ पभादपुण्णिमाचन्दो विअ पण्डुरपरिक्खीणो चिट्ठदि ।

उभौ । (परिक्रम्य उपसृत्य च) जअदु जअदु महाराओ ।

राजा । वअस्स [4]कहं पुणो विअक्खणाए मिलिदो-सि ।

विदूषकः । अज्ज विअक्खणा मए सह सन्धिं कादुं आअदा । किदसन्धीए एदाए सह मन्तअन्तस्स [5]एत्तिआ वेला लग्गा ।

राजा । [6]सन्धिकरणस्स किं फलं ।

विदूषकः । एसा अहिमदजणपेसिदलेहहत्था जं [7]विअक्खणा आगदा ।

1. K अइ, W अय. 2. W *add.* कप्पूरमंजरीए महाराय-संणिहिदा पेसिदा तुमं. 3. K मअक्खामो, W मयजलक्खामो. 4. K कहं, W कहिं. 5. K एत्तिआ, W एदा. 6. K ०करणस्स, W ०कारणस्स. 7. W वियक्खणागदा.

राजा। (गन्धं सूचयित्वा) केदईकुसुमगन्धो विअ।

विचक्षणा। केदईदललेहो एसो मह हत्थे।

राजा। महुसमए किं केदईकुसुमं।

विचक्षणा। [1]भइरवाणन्ददिण्णतन्तप्पहावेण देवीए भवणुज्जाणे [2]केदईलट्ठीए एक्को दाव पसवो दंसिदो। तस्य दोहिं दलसम्पुडेहिं अज्ज हिण्डोलअपभञ्जणीए चउत्थीए हरवल्लहाए देवीए देवी अच्चिदा। अण्णं च दलसम्पुडजुअलं पुण कणिट्ठबहिणिआए कप्पूरमञ्जरीए पसादीकदं। तीए वि एक्केण दलसम्पुडेण भअवदी गोरी ज्जेव अच्चिदा। अण्णं च

[3]केदईकुसुमपत्तसम्पुडं पाहुडं तुह सहीएँ पेसिदं।
एणणाहिमसिवण्णसोहिणा जं सिलोअजुअलेण लंछिदं ॥७॥

(लेखं समर्पयति)।

राजा। (प्रसार्य वाचयति)

हंसिं कुङ्कुमपङ्कपिञ्जरतणुं काऊण जं वञ्चिदो
तब्भत्ता किल चक्कवाअघरणी एस-त्ति मण्णन्तओ।
एदं तं मह दुक्किदं परिणदं दुक्खाणं सिक्खावणं
एक्कत्थो-वि ण जासि जेण विसअं दिट्ठीतिहाअस्स-वि ॥८॥

राजा [तदेव] [4]द्विस्त्रिर्वाचयति।

विदूषकः। एदाइं ताइं [5]मअणरसाअणाइं अक्खराइं।

---

1. K °दिण्ण°, W °विम्भम°. 2. K केदई°, W केअई°. 3. K °कुसुम°, WR °कुसम°. 4. W °स्त्रि वाचयता. 5. RW मअअरसाअणक्खराइं.

विचक्षणा। [1]दुदिओ उण मए पिअसहीए अवत्थाणिवेदओ कदुअ सिलोओ लिहिदो एत्थ।

राजा। (वाचयति)

सह [2]दिवसणिसाहिं दीहरा सासदण्डा
सह मणिवलएहिं बाहधारा गलन्ति।
तुह सुहअ [3]विओए तीएँ [4]उब्बिम्बिरीए
सह-अ तणुलदाए दुब्बला जीविदासा॥ ९॥

विचक्षणा। इह ज्जेव एदाए अवत्थाए मह महल्लबहिणिआए सुलक्खणाए [5]ओलग्गा भविअ सिलोगो कदो तं महाराओ सुणदु[6]।

णीसासा हारजट्ठीसरिसपसरणा चन्दणुच्चोडकारी
चण्डो देहस्स दाहो [7]सुमरणसरणा हाससोहा मुहम्मि।
अङ्गाणं पण्डुभावो दिवहससिकलाकोमलो[8] किं-च तीए
णिच्चं बाहप्पवाहा तुह सुहअ कदे होन्ति कुल्लाहि तुल्ला॥

राजा। (निश्वस्य) किं भण्णइ। [9]कइत्तणेण तुह जेट्ठबहिणिआ[10] खु सा।

विदूषकः। एसा विअक्खणा महीअलसरस्सई। एदाए उण जेट्ठबहिणिआ तिहुअणसरस्सई। ता एदाहिं समं पाडिसिद्धिं

---

1. K दुद्दिओ, W दुविउ. 2. K दिवस०, W दिवस्स०. 3. K विओए, W विउए. 4. K उब्बि०, W उव्वि०. 5. K ओलग्गा० W उलग्गभवीआ०. 6. W सुणेदु. 7. K सुमरण० W समरण०. 8. K ०कोमलो, W ०कोमला. 9. OR सुकइत्तणेण, W सुकयत्तणेण, K कइत्तणे. 10. K ०बहिणिआ, W ०बिहिणिआ.

ण करिस्सं। किं पुण पिअवस्सस्स पुरदो मअणावत्थं अत्तणो उचिदेहिं[1] अक्खरेहिं णिवेदेमि।

विचक्षणा। पढ[2]। एदं सुणीअदि।

विदूषकः।

परं जोण्हा [3]उण्हा गरलसरिसो चन्दणरसो
[4]खरक्खारो हारो रअणिपवणा देहतवणा।
मुणाली बाणाली जलइ-अ जलद्दा तणुलदा
वरिट्ठा जं॰दिट्ठा कमलवअणा सा सुणअणा ॥११॥

राजा। वअस्स ता तुमं-पि [5]थोएण चन्दणरसेण समालिहिअसि। ता कहेसु तग्गदं किं-पि वत्तं। अध अन्तेउरे णइअ देवीए किं किदं तिस्सा।

विदूषकः। विअक्खणे किं किदं। 12

विचक्षणा। मण्डिदा टिक्किदा भूसिदा तोसिदा-अ।

राजा। कधं [6]विअ।

विचक्षणा। [7]घणमुव्वट्टिदमङ्गं कुङ्कुमरसपङ्कपिञ्जरं तिस्सा।

राजा। रोसाणिअं फुडं ता कञ्चणमअबालिआरूवं ॥ १२ ॥ 16

विचक्षणा। मरगअमञ्जीरजुअं चरणा से लम्भिआ वअंसीहिं।

राजा। भमिअमहोमुहपङ्कअजुअलं ता भमरमालाए ॥ १३ ॥

---

1. CORT उचिदेहिं, W उच्चिदेहं. 2. K पढ, W पढइ. 3. W *om.* उण्हा. 4. W खरंखा॰, K खदक्खा॰. 5. K थोएण, W थोवेण. 6. W वियक्खणे *for* विअ. 7. P ॰मुव्वद्दिद, W ॰मुव्वड्ढिद.

विचक्षणा। [1]राअसुअपिच्छणीलं पट्टंसुअजुअलअं णिअत्था सा।
राजा। कअलीएँ [2]कन्दली ता खरपवणपणोल्लिअदलग्गा ॥१४॥
विचक्षणा। तीए णिअम्बफलए णिवेसिआ पोमराअमणिकञ्ची।
राजा। कञ्चणसेलसिलाए बरही ता कारिओ णट्टं ॥१५॥
विचक्षणा। दिण्णा [3]वलआवलीओ करकमलपओट्ठणालजुअलम्मि।
राजा। ता [4]भण किं ण-हि रेहइ विवरीअं मअणतोणीरं ॥१६॥
विचक्षणा। कण्ठम्मि तीएँ ठविदो छम्मासअमोत्तिआण वरहारो।
राजा। सेवइ ता पंतीहिं मुहचन्दं तारआणिअरो ॥ १७ ॥
विचक्षणा। [5]उहएसु वि सवणेसुं णिवेसिअं रअणकुण्डलजुअं से।
राजा। ता वअणमम्महरहो दोहि वि चक्केहिँ चङ्कमिदो ॥१८
विचक्षणा। जञ्जञ्जणजणिदपसाहणाइँ तीए कआइँ णअणाइं।
राजा। ता [6]उप्पण्णे णअकुवलअसिलिम्मुहे पञ्चबाणस्स ॥१९॥
विचक्षणा। कुडिलालआण माला ललाडलोलग्गसाङ्गिणी [7]रइआ।
राजा। ता ससिबिम्बस्सोवरि वट्टइ मज्झाओ सारङ्गो ॥२०॥
विचक्षणा। [8]घणसारतारणअणाएँ गूढकुसुमुच्चओ चिहुरभारो।
राजा। ससिराहुमल्लजुज्झं-व[9] दंसिदमेणणअणाए ॥ २१ ॥
विचक्षणा। इअ [10]देवीएँ जहिच्छिअपसाहणेहिं पसाहिआ कुमरी।
राजा। ता केलिकाणणमही विहूसिआ सुरहिलच्छीए ॥२२॥

---

1. K पिच्छ, W पिंछ. 2. K कन्दली ता, W कंदलया. 3. K वलआवलीउ, W वलयालीउ. 4. W किं न हि, K किं ण. 5. K उहएसुं, W उहएस. 6. W उप्पणे. 7. K रइआ, W रईआ. 8. K घणसारतारणअणाइ, W घणसारमंजरीए. 9. P व, W वं. 10. W देवीइ.

विचक्षणा। देव इदं परमत्थं विण्णवीअदि

जिस्सा दिट्ठी सरलधवला कज्जलं [1]तीएँ जोग्गं
जा वित्थिण्णत्थणकलसिणी रेहइ [1]तीएँ हारो।
चक्काआरे रमणफलए को-वि [2]कञ्चीमरट्टो
जिस्सा तिस्सा पुण पभणिमो भूसणं दूसणं-च ॥२३॥

राजा। (पुनस्ताम् अनुसन्धाय)

तिवलिवलिअणाहीबाहुमूलेसु लग्गं
[3]थणकलसणिअम्बाडम्बरेसूसन्तं।
जलणिविडमिमीएं [4]लण्हअं ण्हाणपोत्तं
पिसुणदि तणुलच्छीलङ्गिमं चङ्गिमं-च ॥२४॥

विदूषकः। (सक्रोधमिव) भो मए सव्वालंकिदा [5]वण्णिदा। तुमं पुण जलविलुत्तपसाहणं जेव [6]सुमरसि। ता किं ण सुदं देवेण णिसग्गचङ्गस्स-वि माणुसस्स सोहा समुम्मीलदि भूसणेहिं। मणीणं जच्चाणं-वि कञ्चणेण विभूसणे लब्भादि का-वि लच्छी ॥२५

राजा। मुद्धाण णाम हिअआइँ हरन्ति हन्त
णेवच्छकप्पणगुणेण णिअम्बिणीओ।
छेआ पुणो पअइचङ्गिमभाविणिज्जा
दक्खारसो ण महुरज्जदि सक्कराए ॥ २६ ॥

विचक्षणा। जधा देवेण दिट्ठं

थोराणं थणआण कण्णकलिआलङ्घीण अच्छीण वा
भूचन्दस्स कन्तिसरिआसोत्तस्स गत्तस्स-अ।

---

1. STU तीए, W तीइ. 2. K ०मरट्ठो, W ०रमट्ठो. 3. K ०रेसूसन्तं, W ०रेसुससंभं. 4. K लण्हअं, W लण्हयं. 5. K वण्णिदा, W विण्णिदा. 6. K सुमरसि, W समरसि.

को णेवच्छकलाएँ कीरदि गुणो जं तं-पि सव्वं पिअं
सुत्तव्वं सुण तत्थ कारणमिमं रूढीएँ का खण्डणा ॥२७

राजा। सुप्पञ्जल कविञ्जल एस सिक्खावीअसि।

किं कज्जं कित्तिमेणं विरअणविहिणा सो णडीणं विडम्बो
तं चङ्गं जं णिसग्गं जणमणहरणं तेण सीमन्तिणीओ।
जस्सिं सव्वङ्गसङ्गो सअलगुणगणो सो अदम्भो अलम्भो
तस्सिं णेच्छन्ति काले परमसुहअरे किं-पि णेवच्छलच्छि॥

विचक्षणा। [1]देव इदं विण्णवीअदि। ण केवलं देवीणिअमेण तिस्सा अनुगद-म्हि। [2]तारामेत्तीए-वि सहित्तणं उवगदा कप्पूर-मञ्जरीए। तेण तक्कज्जसज्जा अहं पुण [3]ओलग्गाविआ भविस्सं।

तिस्सा तावपरिक्खिणाएँ णिहिदो हत्थो थणुत्थङ्गदो
[4]दाहुड्डामरिदो सहीहि बहुसो हेलाएँ कड्ढिज्जदि।
किं तेणावि इमं णिसामअ गिरं [5]सन्तोसणिं तासणिं
हत्थच्छत्तणिवारिदेन्दुकिरणा बोलेइ सा जामिणिं ॥२९॥

कज्जसेसं कविञ्जलओ णिवेदइस्सदि। तं च [6]तधा कादव्वं।

इति परिक्रम्य निष्क्रामति

राजा। (सरभसम् उपसृत्य विदूषकं प्रति) किं पुण तं कज्जसेसं।

विदूषकः। अज्ज [7]हिन्दोलअचउत्थी। तहिं गोरिं कदुअ देवीए कप्पूरमञ्जरी हिन्दोलए आरोइदव्वा। ता [8]मरगअपुञ्जट्ठिदेण

---

1. W *om.* देव. 2. K तारामित्तीए, W तारयमित्तीए. 3. K ओलग्गा०, W उलग्गा०. 4. K ०ड्डामरिदो, W ०डामरिदो. 5. K सन्तोसणं, W संतोसणं. 6. K तधा, W तए. 7. K ०चदुत्थी, W ०चउत्थीए. 8. K ०पुञ्जट्ठिदेण, W ०पुंजिट्ठिदेण.

ज्जेव देवेण कप्पूरमञ्जरी [1]हिन्दोलअन्ती दट्ठव्वा। एदं तं कज्जसेसं।

राजा। (विचिन्त्य) ता अइणिउणा-वि [2]छलिदा देवी। पाइआ [3]जुण्णमज्जारिआ दुद्धं-त्ति तक्कं। (विदूषकं प्रति) वअस्स को अण्णो तुम्हाहिंतो मे कज्जसज्जो। को अण्णो चन्दाहिंतो [4]समुद्दवड्ढणणिट्ठो।

इति परिक्रम्य कदलीगृहप्रवेशं नाटयति।

विदूषकः। इअं अच्चुत्तमा फलिहमणिवेदिआ। ता इह उपविसदु वअस्सो।

राजा तथा करोति।

विदूषकः। (हस्तम् उद्यम्य) भो दीसदु पुण्णिमा-[5]इन्दु।

राजा। (विलोक्य स्वगतं) अहो दोलारूढाए मह वल्लहाए वअणं [6]पुण्णिमा-इन्दु-त्ति णिद्दिसदि। (सम्यग् अवलोक्य)

विच्छाअन्तो [7]णअररमणीमण्डलस्साणणाइं
[8]विच्छालेन्तो गअणकुहरं कन्तिजोण्हाजलेण।
पेच्छन्तीणं हिअणिहिदं णिद्दलन्तो-अ दप्पं
दोलालीलासरलतरलो दीसदे से मुहेन्दू ॥३०॥

अवि-अ

उच्चेहिं गोउरेहिं धुअधवलवडाडम्बरिल्लावलीहिं
घण्टाहिं विन्दुरिल्लासुरतरुणिविमाणाणुसारं लहन्ती।

---

1. K हिन्दोलअन्ती, W हिन्दोवाअयंती. 2. K छलिदा, W छलिदा. 3. K जुण्णमज्जा०, W जुण्णमंजा०. 4. K ०वड्ढणणिट्ठो, W ०वड्ढणतणिट्ठो. 5. W ०इंदो. 6. C ०इंदु, W ०इंद. 7. K ०स्साणणाइं, W ०साणणाइं. 8. W विच्छालिंती.

पाआरं लङ्घअन्ती कुणदि रअवसा उण्णमन्ती णमन्ती
एन्ति जन्ति-अ दोला जणमणहरणी बुड्डणुब्बुड्डणेहिं ॥

अवि-अ

रणन्तमणिणेउरं झणझणन्तहारच्छडं
कणक्कणिदकिङ्किणीमुहरमेहलाडम्बरं ।
विलोलवलआवलीजणिदमञ्जुसिञ्जारवं
ण कस्स मणमोहणं ससिमुहीएँ हिन्दोलणं ॥३२॥

विदूषकः । भो सुत्तआरो तुवं । अहं पुण वित्तिआरो भविअ वित्थरेण वण्णेमि ।

राजा ।

उवरिट्ठिअथणप्पब्भारचम्पिअं चरणपङ्कआण जुअं ।

विदूषकः ।

[1]पुक्कारइ-व्व मअणं रणन्तमणिणेउररवेण ॥३३॥

राजा ।

[2]हिन्दोलणलीलालल‌णलम्पडं रहचक्कचक्कलं रमणं ।

विदूषकः ।

[3]किलकिलइ-व्व सहरिसं [4]कञ्चीमणिकिङ्किणिरवेण ॥३४॥

राजा ।

तारन्दोलणहेलासरन्तसरिअच्छलेण से हारो ।

विदूषकः ।

[5]विक्किरइ-व कुसुमाउहणरवइणो कित्तिवल्लीओ ॥३५॥

राजा ।

[6]सम्मुहपवणपणोल्लिअवरिल्लदरदाविआइँ अङ्गाइं ।

---

1. W पुक्कारयव्व. 2. P ०लीलाचलणलम्पडं. 3. K किलकिलइ, W किलकिलिइ. 4. K कंचमणि, W मणिकञ्ची. 5. K विक्किरइ, W विक्खिरइ. 6. K संमुहपवण, W सम्मुपवण.

विदूषकः ।

[1]हक्कारिऊण मअणं पासम्मि [2]णिवेसअन्ति-व्व ॥ ३६ ॥

राजा ।

ताडङ्कजुअं गण्डेसु बहलघुसिणेसु घडणलीलाहिं ।

विदूषकः ।

देइ-व दोलन्दोलणरेहाओ [3]गणणकोड्डेण ॥ ३७ ॥

राजा ।

णअणाइँ पसइसरिसाइँ झत्ति फुल्लाइँ कोदुहल्लेण ।

विदूषकः ।

[4]अप्पेन्ति-व [5]कुवलअदलसिलिम्मुहे पञ्चबाणस्स ॥३८॥

राजा ।

दोलारअविच्छेओ कहं-पि मा होहि इत्ति पडइ-व्व ।

विदूषकः ।

पिट्ठिम्मि वेणिदण्डो वम्महचम्मट्ठिआअन्तो ॥ ३९ ॥

राजा ।

इअ [6]एदाएँ विलासुज्जलाइँ दोलापवञ्चचरिआइं ।

विदूषकः ।

कस्स ण लिहइ-व चित्ते णिउणं कन्दप्पचित्तअरो ॥४०॥

राजा । (सविषादम्) [7]अवइण्णा कप्पूरमञ्जरी । रित्ता दोला । रित्तं मज्झ चित्तं । रित्ताइं दंसणुस्सुअजणणअणाइं ।

विदूषकः । ता [8]विज्जुलेह-व्व खणदिट्ठणट्ठा ।

राजा । मा एवं भण । [9]हरिअन्दपुरि-व्व दिट्ठा पणट्ठा-अ ।

---

1. K ०उण, W ०उ-व्व. 2. K ०सअन्ति, W सिअन्ति. 3. K गणण, W गगण. 4. K अप्पेन्ति-व, W अप्पन्ति-व्व. 5. K सिलीमुहे, W सिलिंमुहे. 6. STU एदाए, W एमाइ. 7. CPORT अवइणा, W अवयणा. 8. W -इव for -व्व. 9. K हरिचन्दपुरी विअ, W हरयंद-पुव्वरि-व्व.

(स्मृतिनाटितकेन)

मञ्जिट्ठी ओट्ठमुद्दा णवघडिअसुवण्णुज्जला अङ्गलट्ठी
दिट्ठी वालिन्दुलेहाधवलिमजअणी कुन्तला कज्जलाभा ।
इत्थं वण्णाणं रेहा विअरइ हरिणीचञ्चलच्छीएँ एसा
कन्दप्पो जाअदप्पो जगजणजअणे वद्धलक्खुट्ठआदि ॥४१॥

विदूषकः । एदं तं मरगअपुञ्जं । इह उपविसिअ पिअवअस्स पडिवालेदु तं । सञ्झा-वि सण्णिहिदा ज्जेव वट्टदि । (तथा कुरुते)

राजा । (स्मरणम् अभिनीय) अइसिसिरं-पि हिमाणिं सन्तावदाइणिं मज्झण्णवेलं अणुहवामि ।

विदूषकः । ता लच्छीसहअरो खणं चिट्ठदु देवो जाव अहं सिसिरोवआरसामग्गिं संपाडेमि । (इति नाट्येन निष्क्रम्य पुरो विलोक्य च) किं पुण विअक्खणा इदो णिअडिआ आगच्छदि ।

राजा । सण्णिहिदो [1]संकेदकालो कहिदो मन्तीहिं-पि (स्मृत्वा मदनाकूतम् अभिनीय)

किसलअकरचरणा-वि-हु कुवलअणअणा मिअङ्कवअणा-वि ।
अहह णवचम्पअङ्गी तह-वि-हु तावेइ अच्चरिअं ॥४२॥

विदूषकः । (सम्यग् विलोक्य) अहो विअक्खणा सिसिरोवआरसामग्गिसहिदा आअदा ।

ततः प्रविशति गृहीतशिशिरोपचारसामग्री विचक्षणा ।

विचक्षणा । (परिक्रम्य) अहो पिअसहीए विरहदाहज्जरो ।

विदूषकः । (उपसृत्य) [2]भोदी किं एदं ।

---

1. K संकेद०, W संकेय०. 2. K भोदि, W भादि.

विचक्षणा । सिसिरोवआरसामग्गी ।

विदूषकः । कस्स कदे ।

विचक्षणा । पिअसहीए कदे ।

विदूषकः । ता मज्झं-पि अद्धं देहि ।

विचक्षणा । किं णिमित्तं ।

विदूषकः । महाराअस्स कदे ।

विचक्षणा । किं-पुण कारणं ।

विदूषकः । कप्पूरमञ्जरीए-वि किं ।

विचक्षणा । किं ण [1]जांणसि महाराअस्स दंसणं ।

विदूषकः । तुवं-पि किं ण जाणासि महाराअस्स कप्पूरमञ्जरीए दंसणं । (इत्युभौ[2] हसतः)

विचक्षणा । ता कहिं महाराओ ।

विदूषकः । तुह वअणेण मरगअपुञ्जे चिट्ठदि ।

विचक्षणा । ता महाराएण सह मरगअपुञ्जदुआरे चिट्ठ जेण उहअदंसणे जादे सिसिरोआरसामग्गीए जलञ्जली दिज्जदि ।

विदूषकः । (ताम् उपसृत्य) तहिं गच्छ जदो णागच्छसि[3] (इति क्षिपति । तां प्रति) ता कीस तीए दुआरदेसे भविदव्वं ।

विचक्षणा । देवीए आदेसेण ।

विदूषकः । किं तीए आदेसो ।

विचक्षणा । तहिं देवीए [4]बालतरुआ तिण्णि आरोविदा ।

विदूषकः । के के ।

---

1. W याणसि. 2. K उभौ. W उभे. 3. CP नागच्छसि, W णागच्छदि. 4. N ०तरुआ, W ०तरू.

विचक्षणा । कुरुवअतिलअअसोआ ।

विदूषकः । ता किं तेहिं ।

विचक्षणा । भणिदा सा देवीए [1]जधा

कुरुवअतिलअअसोआ आलिङ्गणदंसणग्गचलणहआ ।
विअसन्ति सुन्दरीणं [2]ता ताणं देहि दोहलअं ॥ ४३ ॥

एण्हिं तं संपाडइस्सदि ।

विदूषकः । ता मरगअपुञ्जादो पिअवअस्सं आणिअ तमालविडवन्तरिअं ठविअ एदं पच्चक्खं [3]करइस्सं । (तथा नाटयित्वा राजानं प्रति) भो भो उट्ठिअ संपेक्ख णिअहिअअसमुद्दचन्दलेहं ।

राजा तथा करोति ।

ततः प्रविशति विशेषभूषिताङ्गी[4] कर्पूरमञ्जरी ।

कर्पूरमञ्जरी । कहिं पुण विअक्खणा ।

विचक्षणा । (ताम् उपसृत्य) [5]सहि कीरदु [6]देवीए समादिट्ठं ।

राजा । वअस्स किं-पुण तं ।

विदूषकः । तमालविडवन्तरिदो भविअ जाण ।

विचक्षणा । एस कुरुवअतरू ।

कर्पूरमञ्जरी तम् आलिङ्गति ।

1. W *om.* जधा. 2. W *om.* ता. 3. K करइस्सं, W करिइस्सं. 4. POR °भूषितांगी, W °भूतांगी. 5. CPOR कीरदु, W कीरउ. 6. K देवीए, W देवी°.

राजा । णवकुरुवअरुक्खो कुम्भथोरत्थणीए
रहसविरइदेणं णिब्भरालिङ्गणेणं ।
तह [1]कुसुमसमिद्धिं लम्भिदो सुन्दरीए
जह भसलकुलाणं एत्थ जत्ता समत्ता ॥४४॥

विदूषकः । भो भो [2]पेक्ख महेन्दजालं । जेण
बालो-वि कुरुवअतरू तरुणीए गाढमवगूढो ।
सहस-त्ति कुसुमणिअरं मअणसरं विअ समुग्गिरइ ॥४५॥

राजा । ईदिसो जेव दोहलस्स पहावो ।

विचक्षणा । अअं तिलअद्दुमो ।

कर्पूरमञ्जरी [3]चिरं तिर्यग् अवलोकयति ।

राजा ।

तिक्खाणं तरलाण कज्जलकलासंवग्गिदाणं-पि से
पासे पञ्चसरं सिलीमुहधरं णिच्चं कुणन्ताण-अ ।
णेत्ताणं तिलअद्दुमे णिवडिदा धाडी मअच्छिएँ जं
तं सो मञ्जरिपुञ्जदन्तुरसिरो रोमञ्चिदो [4]वट्टादि ॥४६॥

विचक्षणा । [5]एसो-वि असोहसाही ।

कर्पूरमञ्जरी चरणेन ताडयति ।

राजा ।

असोअतरुताडणं रणिदणेउरेणांहिणा
कदं च मअलञ्छणच्छविमुहीएँ हेलुलसं ।

---

1. K कुसुम॰, W कुसम॰. 2. K पेक्ख, W पिक्ख. 3. W *om.*
4. N वड्ढदि, W वट्टिदि. 5. K एसो, W एसे.

सिहासु सअलासु-वि [1]त्थवअमण्डणाडम्बरं
[2]ठिदं गअणङ्गणे [3]जणणिरिक्खणिज्जं खणं ॥४७॥

विदूषकः । भो वअस्स जं सअं ण कदं दोहलदाणं देवीए एत्थ [4]जाणसि किं कारण ।

राजा । तुवं [4]जाणसि ।

विदूषकः । भणामि जदि देवो ण कुप्पदि ।

राजा । को एत्थ रोसावसरो । भण । उम्मुदिदा जीहा ।

विदूषकः ।

इह जइ-वि कामिणीणं सुन्देरं धरइ अवअवाण सिरी ।
अहिदेवएँ-व्व णिवसइ तह-वि-हु तारुण्णऍ तीए ॥४८॥

राजा । मुणिदो-दे अहिप्पाओ । किं-पुण किं-पि भणामो ।

वालाओँ होन्ति कोऊहलेण एमेव [6]चवलचित्ताओ ।
[7]दरोल्लसिअथणीओँ पुण धरन्ति मअरद्धअरहस्सं ॥४९॥

विदूषकः । [8]तरुणो-वि रूअरेहाररहस्सेण फुल्लन्ति । ण उणो रइरहस्सं जाणन्ति ।

(नेपथ्ये) वैतालिकः । सुहसञ्झा भोदु देवस्स ।

लोआणं लोअणेहिं सह कमलवणं अद्धणिद्दं कुणन्तो
मुञ्चन्तो तिव्वभावं सह-अ सहरिसं माणिणिमाणसेहिं ।

---

1. K त्थवअ॰, W त्ववय॰. 2. CPNOS ठिदं, W दिट्ठं. 3. K ॰णिरिक्ख॰, W ॰णिरक्ख॰. 4. COR जाणामि, W जाण. 5. K चवलं, W चलण॰. 6. W दरल्लसिय ठणीउ. 7. K तरुणो, W तारुणो.

मञ्जिट्ठारत्तसुत्तच्छविकिरणचओ चक्कवाएक्कमित्तो
जादो अत्थाचलत्थो उवह दिणमणी पक्कणारिङ्गपिङ्गो ॥५०

राजा । संणिहिदो सञ्झासमयो वट्टदि ।

विदूषकः । [1]संकेदकालो कधिदो बन्दीहिं[2] ।

कर्पूरमञ्जरी । सहि विअक्खणे गमिस्सं दाव । विआलो संपत्तो ।

विचक्षणा । एवं कीरदु ।

इति परिक्रम्य निष्क्रान्ताः सर्वे ।

द्वितीयं जवनिकान्तरं ।

---

1. K संकेद०, W संकेत्थ०. 2. W *add.* पि.

ततः प्रविशति राजा विदूषकश्च ।

राजा । (ताम् अनुसन्धाय)

दूरे किज्जदु चम्पअस्स कलिआ कज्जं हलिद्दीएँ किं
ओल्लोल्लाइ-वि कञ्चणेण [1]गणणा का णाम जच्चेण-वि ।
लावण्णस्स णउग्गदिन्दुमहुरच्छाअस्स तिस्सा पुरो
[2]पच्चग्गेहि-वि केसरस्स कुसुमुक्केरेहिँ किं कारणं ॥१॥

अवि-अ

मरगअमणिगुच्छा हारलट्ठि-व्व तारा
भमरकवलिअन्ता मालईमालिअ-व्व ।
रहसवलिअकण्ठी तीएँ दिट्ठी वरिट्ठा
सवणपहणिविट्ठा माणसं मे पइट्ठा ॥ २ ॥

विदूषकः । भो वअस्स किं तुवं भज्जाजिदो [3]पइ-व्व किं-पि किं-पि कुरुकुराअन्तो चिट्ठसि ।

राजा । वअस्स पिअं [4]सुविणअं दिट्ठं । [5]तं अणुसन्धामि ।

विदूषकः । ता कीदिसं तं कधेदु पिअवअस्सो ।

राजा ।

जाणे पङ्करुहाणणा सुविणए मं केलिसज्जागदं
कान्दोट्टेण तडत्ति ताडिदुमणा हत्थन्तरे संठिदा ।
ता कोड्डेण मए-वि झत्ति गहिदा ढिल्लं वरिल्लञ्चले
तं [6]मोत्तूण गदं च तीएँ सहसा णट्ठा-खु णिद्दा-वि मे ॥३॥

---

1. W *add.* य *to* गणणा. 2. K पच्चग्ग°, W पच्चुग्ग. 3. R पइ, W पिइ. 4. W सविणअं. 5. W तमणुसंधामि. 6. K मोत्तूण, W मत्तूण.

विदूषकः। (स्वगतम्) भोदु एवं दाव। (प्रकाशम्) भो वअस्स अज्ज मए [1]वि सुविणअं दिट्ठं।

राजा। (सप्रत्याशम्) ता कहिज्जदु कीदिसं तं सुविणअं।

विदूषकः। अज्ज [2]सुविणए सुरसरिसोत्ते सुत्तो-म्हि।

राजा। तदो तदो।

विदूषकः। ता हरसिरोवरि दिण्णलीलावआए गङ्गाए पक्खालिदो-म्हि तोएण।

राजा। तदो तदो।

विदूषकः। तदो [3]सरअसमअविरिसिणा जलहरेण जहिच्छं पीदो-म्हि।

राजा। अच्छरिअं अच्छरिअं। तदो तदो।

विदूषकः। तदो चित्ताणक्खत्तगदे [4]भअवदि मत्तण्डे तम्बवण्णीणदीसंगमे समुद्दं गदो सो महामेहो। जाणे अहं-पि तस्स गब्भट्ठिदो गच्छामि।

राजा। तदो तदो।

विदूषकः। तदो तहिं सो थूलजलबिन्दूहिं वरिसिदुं पअट्टो। अहं-च रअणाअरसुत्तिहिं मुत्तासुत्तिणामधेआहिं तो समुप्फाडिअ जलबिन्दूहिं पीदो। ताणं-च दसमासप्पमाणो मुत्ताहलो भविअ गब्भे संठिदो।

राजा। तदो तदो।

---

1. W *om.* वि. 2. W मिवणए. 3. K ०वरिसि०, W ०वरसि०.
4. K भअवदि मत्तण्डे, W भअवं मत्तंडे.

विदूषकः ।

तदो [1]चउस्सट्ठिसु सुत्तिसु ट्ठिदो घणम्बुबिन्दू जिदवंसरोअणो।
सुवत्तुलं णिच्चलमच्छमुज्जलं कमेण पत्तो णवमोत्तिअत्तणं ॥४॥

तदो सो-हं अत्ताणं ताणं गब्भगदं मुत्ताहलत्तणेण मण्णेमि ।

राजा। तदो तदो ।

विदूषकः। तदो परिणदिकाले समुद्दाओ कड्ढिदाओ ताओ सुत्तिओ फाडिदाओ। अहं [2]चदुस्सट्ठिमुत्ताहलत्तणं गदो ठिदो। [3]कीदो च एक्केण सेट्ठिणा सुवण्णलक्खं [4]देइअ ।

राजा। अहो विचित्तदा सुविणअस्स । तदो तदो ।

विदूषकः। [5]तदो तेण आणिअ वेअडिअं विद्धाविदा मोत्तिआ। मम-वि ईसीसि वेअणा समुप्पण्णा ।

राजा। [5]तदो तदो ।

विदूषकः।

तेणं च [6]मुत्ताहलमण्डलेणं एक्केक्कदाए दसमासिएणं ।
एक्कावली लट्ठिकमेण [7]गुच्छा सा संठिदा कोडिसुवण्णमुल्ला ॥५

राजा। तदो तदो ।

विदूषकः। तदो तं करण्डिआए कदुअ साअरदत्तो गदो पञ्चालाहिवस्स सिरिवज्जाउहस्स णअरं कण्णउज्जं णाम। तदो सा विक्किणीदा कोडीए सुवण्णस्स ।

राजा। तदो तदो ।

1. K चउस्स॰, W चउस॰. 2. K चदुस्स॰, W चदुस॰. 3. K कीदो, W कीण्हो. 4. K देइअ, W देय. 5. W *om. this sentence.* 6. K ॰मण्डलेण, W ॰मण्डणेण. 7. K गुच्छा, W गुञ्छा.

विदूषकः। तदो-अ

[1]दट्ठूण थोरत्थणतुङ्गिमाणं एक्कावलीए तह चङ्गिमाणं।
सा तेण दिण्णा दइआएँ कण्ठे रज्जन्ति छेआ समसंगमम्मि ।।६।।

अवि-अ

[2]णहबहलिदजोण्हाणिब्भरे रत्तिमज्झे
[3]कुसुमसरपहारत्तासंमीलिदाणं।
णिहुवणपरिरम्भे णिब्भरुत्तुङ्गपीण-
त्थणकलसणिवेसा पीडिदो-हं विबुद्धो ।।७।।

राजा। (किञ्चिद् विहस्य विचिन्त्य)

[4]सुविणअमेणमसच्चं तं दिट्ठं मेणुसन्धमाणस्स।
पडिसुविणएण तस्स विणिवारणं तुह अभिप्पाओ ।।८।।

विदूषकः। भट्टो ठक्कुरो [5]छुहाकिलन्तो बम्भणो अविणीद-हिअआ बालरण्डा विरहिदो-अ माणुसो मणोरहमोदएहिं अत्ताणं [6]विडम्बेदि। अवि-अ पुच्छामि वअस्सं कस्स एस पहावो।

राजा। पेम्मस्स।

विदूषकः। भो देवीगदे पणअप्परूढे-वि[7] पेम्मे किं-णु कप्पूरमञ्जरिं [8]सव्वङ्गवित्थारिअलोअणो पिअन्तो विअ पलोएसि। किं तत्तो परिहीअमाणगुणा देवी।

राजा। मा एवं भण

1. K दट्ठूण, W तट्ठूण. 2. W ०बहलिद०. 3. K ०सर-पहारुत्तास०, W ०सरहपत्तास०. 4. *See* Note. 5. K क्षुहा, W कुह०. 6. K विडम्बदि, W विडंबेइ. 7. W *om.* वि. 8. K ०वित्थारिअ०, W ०विछारिअ०.

कीए वि संघडदि कस्स-वि पेम्मगण्ठी
एमेअ इत्थ ण-हु कारणमत्थि रूअं ।
चङ्गत्तणं पुणु महिज्जदि जं तहिं-पि
तं दिज्जए पिसुणलोअमुहेसु मुद्दा ॥ ९ ॥

विदूषकः । भो वअस्स [1]किं पुण एदं पेम्मं पेम्मं-ति भणदि ।

राजा । अण्णोण्णमिलिदस्स मिहुणस्स मअरद्धसासणे पणअ-परूढहिअअगण्ठिं [2]पेम्मं-ति छइल्ला भणन्ति ।

विदूषकः । कीदिसो सो ।

राजा ।

जस्सिं विअप्पघडणाइकलङ्कमुक्को
अन्तो मणम्मि सरलत्तणमेइ भावो ।
[3]एक्केक्कअस्स पसरन्तरसप्पवाहो
सिङ्गारवड्ढिअमणोहवदिण्णसारो ॥१०॥

विदूषकः । कधं [4]विअ सो लच्छीआदि ।

राजा ।

जाणं सहाअपसरन्तसलोलदिट्ठी
पेरन्तलुण्ठिअमणाण परोपरेण ।
[5]वड्ढन्तवम्महविइण्णरसप्पसारो
ताणं पआसइ लहू-वि स [6]चित्तभेओ ॥११॥

1. K किं उण, W पुण किं. 2. K पेम्मं, W पेम. 3. W इक्किक्कयस्स. 4. K विअ, W वि च. 5. K ०विइण्ण०, W ०वियण्ण०. 6. K ० भेओ, W ०हेउ.

विदूषकः ।

अन्तो णिविट्ठमणविब्भमडम्बरो जो
सो भण्णए [1]मअणमण्डणमेत्थ पेम्मं ।
दुल्लक्खअं-पि पअडेइ जणो जअम्मि
तं जाणिमो सुबहुलं [2]मअणेन्दजालं ॥१२॥

किं-च जदि चित्तगदं पेम्मं अणुराअं उप्पादेदि ता किं किज्जदि मण्डणाडम्बरबिडम्बणाए ।

राजा । वअस्स सच्चं इणं ।

किं मेहलावलअसेहरणेउरेहिं
किं चङ्गिमाएँ किमु [3]मण्डणडम्बरेहिं ।
तं अण्णमत्थि इह किं-पि णिअम्बिणीणं
जेणं लहन्ति सुहअत्तणमञ्जरीओ ॥ १३ ॥

किं गेअणट्टविहिणा किमु वारुणीए
धूवेण किं [4]अगुरुणो किमु कुङ्कुमेण ।
मिट्ठत्तणे [5]महिअलम्मि ण किंपि अण्णं
[6]रुच्चिस्स अत्थि सरिसं पुणु माणुसस्स ॥१४॥

अवि-अ

जा चक्कवट्टिघरिणी जणगेहिणी जा
पेम्मम्मि ताण ण तिलं-पि विसेसलम्भो ।

1. K ०मेत्थ, W ०मिच्छ. 2. K ०णीन्द०, W ०णिंद०. 3. K ०रेहिं', W ०रेषा. 4. P अगुरुणा, W अगुरणा. 5. K ०अलम्मि, W अलं-पि. 6. K रुच्चिस्स, W त्तरस्स.

[1]जाणे सिरीऍ जइ [2]किज्ञादि को-वि भेदो
माणिक्कभूसणणिअंसणकुङ्कुमेहिं ॥ १५ ॥

किं लोअणेहिँ तरलेहिँ किमाणणेण
चन्दोवमेण सिहिणेहिँ किमुण्णएहिं ।
ता किं-पि अण्णमिह भूवलए णिमित्तं
जेणङ्गणाओ॑ हिअआओ॑ ण उत्तरन्ति ॥१६॥

विदूषकः । एवं णेदं । किं पुण अण्णं-पि मे कधेसु जं कुमारत्तणे माणुसस्स ण मणोज्ञं [3]तस्स-वि तारुण्णएण किं-पि चङ्गत्तणं [4]चडदि ।

राजा । णूणं दुवे इह पआवइणो [5]जअम्मि
जे देहणिम्मवणजोव्वणदाणदक्खा ।
एक्को घडेइ पढमं कुमरीणमङ्गं
कण्डारिऊण पअडेइ पुणो दुईओ ॥ १७ ॥

तेण-अ
[6]समणिबलअकञ्चीणेउरा वेसलच्छी
मरगअमणिमाला गोरिआ हारलट्ठी ।
हिअअहरणमन्तं जोव्वणं कामिणीणं
जअइ मअणकण्डं छट्ठअं लट्ठअं-च ॥ १८ ॥

---

1. K जाणे सिरीप, W जाणे सरीइ. 2. K किज्जइ को-वि, W किज्जदि को-इ. 3. W तस्साावि. 4. K चडदि, W चडइ. 5. K जअम्मि, W जइम्मि. 6. K समणि०, W सुमिण०.

अदो-अ

अङ्गं लावण्णपुण्णं सवणपरिसरे लोअणे [1]फारतारे
[2]वच्छं थोरत्थणिल्लं तिवलिवलइअं मुट्ठिगेज्झं-च मज्झं ।
चक्काआरो निअम्बो तरुणिमसमए किं णु[3] अण्णेण कज्जं
पञ्चेहिं चेअ बाला मअणजअमहावेजअन्तीओ होन्ति ॥१९

(नेपथ्ये[4]) सहि कुरङ्गीए इमिणा सिसिरोवआरेण [5]णलिणि-व्व क्खामिआ किलिस्सामि ।

विस-व्व बिसकन्दली विसहर-व्व हारच्छडा
वअस्समिव अत्तणो किरदि तालविन्ताणिलो ।
तहा-अ करणिग्गअं जलइ जन्तधाराजलं
ण चन्दणमहोसहं हरइ देहदाहं-च मे ॥ २० ॥

विदूषकः । सूदं पिअवअस्सेण । भरिआ कण्णा पीऊस-गण्डूसेण । ता किं अज्ज-वि उवेक्खिआदि घणघम्मेण [6]किलम्मन्ती मुणालिआ, [7]गाढक्कढिअदूसहेण सलिलेण [8]सिञ्चिज्जन्ती केलिकुसुमपुत्तलिआ, छम्मासिअमुत्तिआणं तडत्ति फुट्टन्ती एक्कावली, गण्ठिवण्णअकेआरिआ लूडिज्जन्ती गन्धहरिणएहिं । ता सच्चं सुविणअं ते [9]सम्पण्णं। एहि पविसम्ह। [10]उब्भिज्जदु मअरद्धअपडाअं । पअट्टदु कण्णकुहरम्मि [11]पञ्चमहुङ्काराणं रिञ्छोली । थक्कन्तु बाहप्पवाहा । मन्थरिज्जन्तु णीसासप्पसवा । लहदु लावण्णं पुणण्णवभावं ।

1. K फार०, W झार०. 2. K वच्छं, W वत्थं. 3. K णु, W तु. 4. *See* Note. 5. K णलिणी, W तालिणी. 6. K किलम्मन्ती, W किलिंमंती. 7. K ०क्कढिद०, W ०क्कढिअं०. 8. K सिञ्चिज्जन्ती, W सिचंती. 9. W *om.* 10. K उब्भिज्जदु, W उज्झिदु. 11. K ०राणं, W ०राण.

इति खडक्किकोद्घाटनेन ततः प्रविशति नायिका कुरङ्गिका च ।

नायिका । (ससाध्वसम् आत्मगतम्) [1]अम्मो किं एस [2]गअणङ्गणेहिं [3]अवइण्णो पुण्णिमाहरिणङ्को । किं-वा तुट्ठेण [4]णीलकण्ठेण णिअदेहं लम्भिओ मणोहओ । किं-वा हिअअस्स दुज्जणो णअणाण सज्जणो [5]मं सम्भावेदि । (प्रकाशम्) [6]इदं इन्द्रजालं पेक्खामि ।

विदूषकः । (राजानं हस्ते गृहीत्वा) भोदि सच्चं इन्दजालं सम्पण्णं ।

नायिका लज्जते ।

कुरङ्गिका । सहि कप्पूरमञ्जरि अब्भुट्ठाणेण [7]सम्भावेहि भट्टारअं ।

नायिका उत्थातुम् इच्छति ।

राजा । (हस्ते गृहीत्वा)

उट्ठिऊण थणभारभङ्गुरं मा [8]मिअङ्कमुहि भञ्ज मज्झअं ।
तुज्झ ईदिसणिवेसदंसणे लोअणाण मअणो [9]पसीददु ॥२१॥

अवि-अ

जिस्सा पुरो हरदि णो हरिआललच्छी
रोसाणिअं ण कणअं ण-अ चम्पआइं ।
ताइं सुवण्णकुसुमेहिँ विलोअणाइं
अच्चेमि जेहिँ हरिणच्छि तुमं-सि दिट्ठा ॥२२॥

1. W अम्हि. 2. W गयणंगणेहि. 3. W अवयणो हरिणंक. 4. K णीलकण्ठ°, W णीलयंठ°. 5. W *om.* 6. W *om.* 7. K °वेहि, W °वेह. 8. *See* Note. 9. NOR पसीदद्, W पसीदतु.

विदूषकः। गब्भहरवासेण सेअसलिलसित्तगत्ता संभूदा [1]तत्त-भोदी कप्पूरमञ्जरी। सिचअञ्चलेण [2]विज्जिस्सं दाव। (तथा कुर्वन्) हा हा कहं वरिलञ्चलेण णिव्वाणो पदीवो। (विचिन्त्य स्वगतम्) [3]लीलुज्जाणं जेव गच्छम्ह। (प्रकाशम्) भो अन्धारपणच्चिदं वट्टदि। ता णिक्कमम्ह सुरङ्गामुहेण ज्जेव [4]पमदुज्जाणं दाव।

सर्वे निष्क्रमणं नाटयन्ति।

राजा। (कर्पूरमञ्जरीं करे गृहीत्वा)

मज्झ हत्थठिदपाणिपल्लवा ईसिसञ्चरणचञ्चुरा भव।
जं चिराअ कलहंसमण्डली भोदु केलिगमणम्मि दूहवा॥२३॥

(स्पर्शसुखम् अभिनीय)

जे णवस्स तउसस्स कण्टआ जे [5]कदम्बकुसुमस्स केसरा।
अज्ज तुज्झ करफंससक्खिणो ते हवन्तु णणु णिज्जिआ धुवं॥

(नेपथ्ये) वैतालिकः।

[3]सुहाणुबन्धणो भोदु देवस्स चन्दुज्जोओ
भूगोले तिमिराणुबन्धमलिणे भूमिहरे-व्व ट्ठिदे
सञ्जादा णवभुञ्जपिञ्जरमुही जोण्हाएँ पूव्वा दिसा।
मुञ्चन्तो [7]मुचुकुन्दकेसरसिहासोहाणुकारे करे
चन्दो एक्ककलाकमेण-अ गदो सम्पुण्णबिम्बत्तणं॥२५

अवि-अ

---

1. PN तत्त॰, W तदो. 2. W वज्जिस्सं, SV वीजिस्सं. 3. K ॰ज्जाणं, W ज्जाणे. 4. K पमदु॰, W पमलु॰. 5. K ॰कुसुम॰, W ॰कुसम॰. 6. W सुहण॰, K सुहणि॰. 7. K ॰केसर॰, W ॰केसरि॰.

अकुङ्कुमचन्दणं [1]दसदिसावहूमण्डणं
अकङ्कणमकुण्डलं भुवणमण्डलीभूसणं ।
असोसणममोहणं मअरलञ्छणस्साउहं
मिअङ्ककिरणावली णहअलम्मि पुञ्जीअदि ॥२६॥

विदूषकः । एसा कञ्चणचण्डेण वण्णिदा [2]चन्दुज्जोअलच्छी । ता संपदं माणिक्कचण्डस्सावसरो ।

(नेपथ्ये) द्वितीयो बन्दी ।

डज्झन्तागुरुधूववट्टिवलआ दिज्जन्तदीवुज्जला
लम्बिज्जन्तविचित्तमोत्तिअलदा मुञ्चन्तपारावआ ।
सज्जिज्जन्तमणोज्जकेलिसअणा [3]जम्पन्तदूईसआ
सेज्जुच्छङ्गवलन्तमाणिणिजणा वट्टन्ति सेज्जाहरा ॥२७॥

अवि-अ

देन्ता कप्पूरपूरच्छुरणमिव दिसासुन्दरीणं मुहेसुं
लण्हं जोण्हं किरन्ता भुअणजणमणाणन्दणं चन्दणं-च ।
जुण्णं कन्दप्पकन्दं तिहुअणकलणाकन्दलिल्लं कुणन्तो
जादा एणङ्कपादा [4]सरअजलहरुम्मुक्कधाराणुकारा ॥२८॥

विदूषकः । दिसअवअंसो णहसरहंसो ।
णिहुअणकन्दो वट्टइ चन्दो ॥ २९ ॥

कुरङ्गिका । [1]ससिहररईअ मरट्टो माणिणिमाणघरट्टो ।
णवचम्पअकोअण्डो मअणो जअइ पचण्डो ॥३०॥

1. K ०वहू०, W ०वहू०. 2. K ०ज्जोअलच्छी, W ०ज्जोअच्छली.
3. K जम्पन्त, W जंपंतु. 4. K ०हरुम्मुक्क०, W ०हरोमुक्क०.

(कर्पूरमञ्जरीं प्रति) पिअसहि तए कदं चन्दवण्णणं महाराअस्स पुरदो पढिस्सं ।

कर्पूरमञ्जरी लज्जते । कुरङ्गिका पठति ।

मण्डले ससहरस्स गोरए दन्तपञ्जरविलासचोरए ।
भादि लाञ्छणमओ [1]फुरन्तओ केलिकोइलतुलं धरन्तओ ॥

राजा । अहो कप्पूरमञ्जरीए अहिणवअत्थदंसणं उत्तिविचित्तत्तणं रमणीओ रसणिस्सन्दो-अ । (तां प्रति)

मा कहिं-पि वअणेण [2]विब्भमो होहि इत्ति तुह णूणमिन्दुणा ।
लञ्छणच्छलमसीविसेसओ पेच्छ बिम्बवलए णिए कदो ॥३२॥

किं च

पण्डुरंगि जइ रज्जए मुहं कोमलङ्गि खडिआरसेण दे ।
दिज्जए पुण कवोलकज्जलं ता लहेज्ज ससिणो [3]विडम्बणं ॥३३

(चन्द्रम् उद्दिश्य)

मुक्कसङ्कं हरिणङ्क किं तुवं सुन्दरीपरिसरे हिण्डसि ।
तुज्झ बिम्बपरिपण्डुरत्तणं पेच्छ दिण्णमिमिणा मुहेण दे[4] ॥३४

नेपथ्ये कलकलः । सर्वे आकर्णितकेन

राजा । किं पुण एस महाकोलाहलो ।

कर्पूरमञ्जरी । (ससाध्वसा) पिअसहि एदं अवगमिअ आगच्छ ।

---

1. K फुरन्तओ, W फुरंगउ. 2. K विब्भमो, W विब्भउ. 3. K विड॰, W वेड॰. 4. K दे, W ते.

विदूषकः। देवीए पिअवअस्सस्स वञ्चणाकदं अवगमिअ आअच्छदि। ता कुज्जवामणकिराअवरिसवरसोविदल्लाणं एस हलबोलो।

कर्पूरमञ्जरी। ता मं पेसेदु महाराओ जेण ञ्जेव इहागदा-वि ण जाणीआमि। सुरङ्गामुहेण पविसिअ [1]रक्खाघरं गच्छामि जह देवी महाराएण सह संगमं ण जाणादि[2]।

इति निष्क्रान्ताः सर्वे।

तृतीयं [3]जवनिकान्तरम्।

---

1. K ०घरं, W हरं. 2. W *add.* राजा एवं कुरुमह. 3. K ज्ञवनिका, W यवनिका.

ततः प्रविशति राजा विदूषकश्च ।

राजा । अहो गाढअरो अम्ह-गिम्हो । अहो पवलो मलअ-पवणो । ता कहं सहिदव्वो । जदो

इह कुसुमसरेक्कगोअराणं इदमुभअं-पि हु [1]दूसहं-ति मण्णे ।
जरढरविकरालिदो-अ कालो सुहअजणेण पिएण विप्पलम्भो ॥१॥

विदूषकः । एक्के वम्महवहणिज्जा अण्णे तावसोसणिज्जा । अम्हारिसो जणो ण कामस्स वहणिज्जो ण तावस्स सोसणिज्जो ।

(नेपथ्ये)

शुकः । किं [2]णु खु दे समूलुप्पाडिअचूडिअं सीसं करइस्सं ।

राजा । (विहस्य) वअस्स लीलावणसच्छन्दचारिणा केलीसूएण किं भणिअं ।

विदूषकः । (सक्रोधम्) आ दासीए पुत्त सुलअकरणजुग्गो-सि ।

(नेपथ्ये)

सव्वं तुम्हारिसाहिं-तो संभावीअदि जादि ण मे [3]होन्ति पक्खावलीओ ।

1. दूसहं, W दूसयं. 2. K णु, W म. 3. K होन्ति, W हुन्तीउए.

राजा। कथं उड्डीणो विअ। (विदूषकं प्रति)

णिसा तलिणवित्थरा तह दिणेसु वड्ढत्तणं
ससी लहइ खण्डणं तह अखण्डबिम्बो रई।
णिदाहदिअसेसु [1]विप्फुरइ जस्स एस क्कमो
कहं ण स विही तदो [2]खुरसिहाहि [3]खण्डिज्जइ ॥२॥

किं च णिउणं सेवणिज्जो जदि [4]सुहअसंगमो भोदि। जदो

मज्झण्हे सिरिखण्डपङ्ककलणा आ संझमोल्लंसुअं
लीलामज्जणमा [5]पओससमअं साअं सुरा सीअला।
गिम्हे पच्छिमजामिणीणिहुवणं जं किं-पि पञ्चेसुणो
[6]एदे पञ्चसिलीमुहा विजइणो सेसा सरा जज्जरा ॥३॥

विदूषकः। मा एवं भण।

[7]पण्डुच्छविच्छुरिदणाअलदादलाणं
[8]साहारतेल्लपरिपेसलपोप्फलाणं[9]।
कप्पूरपंसुपरिवासिदचन्दणाणं
भद्दं णिदाहदिवसाण वअस्स भोदु ॥४॥

राजा। इदं पुण एत्थ रमणिज्जं।

सपञ्चमतरङ्गिणो सवणसीअला वेणवो
समं सिसिरवारिणा वअणसीला वारुणी।

---

1. विप्फरइ, W विफुरइ. 2. K ०सिहाहि, W ०सिंहाहिं. 3. K खण्डिज्जइ, W खण्डिज्जदु. 4. K सुहअसंगमो, W सुहिसंगमो. 5. K पओस०, W पउस्स०. 6. NORSTU एदे, W एदी. 7. K पण्डुच्छवि०, W पंडुत्थवि०. 8. K साहार०, W साहार०. 9. K ०पोप्फलाणं, W ०पुफलाणं.

सचन्दणघणत्थणी [1]सअणसीअला कामिणी
णिदाहदिवसोसहं भण ण सीअलं कस्स-वि ॥५॥

अवि-अ

[2]लीलुत्तंसे सिरीसं सिहिणपरिसरे सिन्धुवाराण हारो
अङ्गे ओल्लं वरिल्लं रमणपणइणी मेहला उप्पलेहिं ।
दोसुं दोकन्दलीसुं णवबिसवलआ कामविज्ञो [3]मणोज्ञो
[4]तावातङ्केक्कतन्तं महुसमअगदे एस वेसो-बलाणं ॥६॥

विदूषकः । अहं पुण भणामि

मज्झण्हसण्हघणचन्दणपङ्किलाणं
साअं णिवेसिअणिरन्तरमज्जणाणं ।
सामासु वीअणवारिकणुक्खिदाणं
दासत्तणं कुणदि पञ्चसरो [5]वहूणं ॥७॥

राजा । (स्मरणम् अभिनीय)

[6]पञ्चग्गं णवरूवभङ्गिघडणारम्मे जणे संगमं
[7]जाणं ताणँ खणं-व रत्तिदिअहा गच्छान्ति दीहा अवि ।
जाणं ते-अ मणं-पि देन्ति ण रइं चित्तस्स सन्ताविणो
ताणं जन्ति मणोरहेक्कजणणा मासोवमा वासरा ॥८॥

(विदूषकं प्रति) अवि-अ अत्थि तग्गदा का-वि वत्ता ।

1. PNR सयण०, W सायस०. 2. K लीलु०, W लीलो०. 3. W मणुज्जी. 4. K ०तङ्केक्क०, W ०तंकिक्क०. 5. K वहूणं, W वहूणं. 6. K पञ्चग्गं, W पंचग्गं. 7. जाणं ताणं etc., W वंकलाव मणम्मि होंति सयसा जे णाम इल्लोहलो.

विदूषकः। अत्थि। सुणदु वअस्स। कहेमि[1] सुहासिअं ते। जा सा कप्पूरमञ्जरीए रक्खाभवणे सुरङ्गा दिण्णा सा देवीए दिट्ठा।

राजा। तदो तदो।

विदूषकः। तदो सुरङ्गदुआरं पिहुलसिलासञ्चएण णिरन्धं करिअ णिबद्धं। अण्णं च अणङ्गसेणा कलिङ्गसेणा कामसेणा वसन्तसेणा विब्भमसेण-त्ति पञ्चचामरधारिणीओ सेण-त्ति णामधेआ सद्देण फरक्किदफरआ करवालहत्था सहचारणीओ कारामन्दिरस्स रक्खाणिमित्तं पुव्वदिसाए णिउत्ताओ। अणङ्गलेहा चन्दणलेहा चित्तलेहा [2]मिअङ्कलेहा विब्भमलेह-त्ति णामधेआओ पञ्चसेरन्धीओ पुंखिदसिलिमुहधणुहत्था[3] दक्खिणदिसाए णिवेसिदाओ। कुन्दमाला चन्दमाला चन्दणमाला मङ्गलमाला काञ्चणमाल-त्ति णामधेआओ तह कलिदकुन्तहत्थाओ तम्बोलकरण्डवाहिणीओ पच्छिमदिसाए ठविदाओ। अणङ्गकेली चक्करकेली सुन्दरकेली राअकेली कन्दप्पकेलीणामधेआओ [4]फडअचक्कवेल्लणविज्जुरिल्ला मज्जणपालीओ केलीसद्देण उत्तरदिसाए आढत्ताओ। ताणं पि पुण मज्झे मन्दरवदी कल्लोलवदी तरङ्गवदी मदिरावदी केलिवदी-त्ति णामधेआओ कणअवेत्तदण्डहत्थाओ सुहासिअपढिआओ [5]अज्झक्खीकदाओ।

राजा। अहो देवीए सामग्गी अन्तेउरोचिदा।

---

1. K सुहासिदं, W कधसुहासिअं. 2. K मिअङ्क॰, W मियंग॰.
3. W *add.* मिसिडसंनज सेरंधीसत्थीण. 4. OR फडयचक्कवेल्लणविज्जुरिल्ला, W फडयकाडयल्लचित्तला विज्जुविदुरिल्लाउ. 5. K अज्झक्खी॰, W अद्दक्खी॰.

विदूषकः । एसा देवीए सारङ्गिआ णाम सही किमपि विण्णविदुं पेसिदा ।

ततः प्रविशति सारङ्गिका ।

सारङ्गिका । जअदु जअदु महाराअ । भट्टारकं देवी विण्णवेदि अज्ज वडसावित्तीमहूसवोवअरणाइं केलिविमाणं आरुहिअ देवेण [1]प्रेक्खिदव्वाइं-त्ति ।

राजा । जं आदिसदि देवी ।

चेटी निष्क्रान्ता । उभे प्रासादाधिरोहणं नाटयतः ।

ततः प्रविशति चर्चरी ।

विदूषकः ।

मुत्ताहलिल्लाहरणोच्चआओ लासावसाणे तलिणंसुआओ ।
[1]सिञ्चन्ति अण्णोण्णमिमीओ॑ पेच्छ जन्तजलेणं मणिभाइणेहिं ॥९

इदो-अ

परिब्भमन्तीओ॑ विचित्तबन्धं इमाओ॑ दोसोलह णच्चणीओ ।
खेलन्ति तालाणुगदप्पआओ तुहङ्गणे दीसदि दण्डरासो ॥१०॥

समंससीसा समबाहुहत्था रेहाविसुद्धा अवराओ॑ देन्ति ।
पंतीहिँ दोहिं लअतालबन्धं परोप्परं साहिमुही चलन्ति ॥११॥

मोत्तूण अण्णा मणिवारआईं जन्तेहि धारासलिलं खिवन्ति ।
पडन्ति ताओ सहिआणमङ्गे [2]मणोभुवो वारुणबाणचङ्गा ॥१२॥

---

1. K पेक्खिदव्वाइं'त्ति, W पिक्खिदव्वमिमित्ति. 2. K सिञ्चन्ति, W सिंचिंति. 3. K ०भुवो, W ०हुवा.

इमा मसीकज्जलकालकाआ तिकण्डचावाओँ विलासिणीओ।
[1]पुलिन्दरूवेण जणस्स हासं समोरपिच्छाहरणा कुणन्ति ॥१३॥

हत्थे [2]महामंसबलीधराओ हुंकारफेक्काररवा रउद्दा।
[3]णिसाअरीणं पडिसीसएहिं अण्णा मसाणाभिणअं कुणन्ति ॥१४॥

का-वि वाइदकरालहुडुक्का मन्दमद्दलल‍एण मिअच्छि।
[4]दोल्लदाहिँ परिचाडिचलाहिं चल्लिकम्मकरणम्मि पअट्टा ॥१५॥

किङ्किणिकदरणज्झणसद्दं कण्ठगीदिलअजन्तिदतालं।
जोइणीवलअणच्चणकेलिं तालणेउररवा विरअन्ति ॥१६॥

कोदुहल्लजङ्गमवेसा वेणुवादणपरा अवराओ।
कालवेसवसभामिअलोआ ओसरन्ति पणमन्ति हसन्ति ॥१७॥

प्रविश्य

सारङ्गिका। (पुरो विलोक्य) एस महाराओ मरगदपुञ्जादो कअलीघरअं अणुपविट्ठो। ता देवीए विण्णविदं विण्णवेमि। (उपसृत्य) जअदु जअदु भट्टा। देवी विण्णवेदि जधा साअंसमए तुम्हे परिणाविदव्व-त्ति।

विदूषकः। भोदि किं एदं अकण्डकुम्हण्डपडणं।

राजा। सारङ्गिए सवित्थरं कहेसु किं ण्णेदं-ति।

सारङ्गिका। एदं विण्णवीआदि। अदिक्कन्तचउद्दसीदिअसे देवीए पोम्मराअमाणिक्कमअं गोरिं कदुअ भइरवाणन्दस्स पासे

---

1. K ०रुवेण, W ०रूपेण. 2. K ०धराओ, W धरीओ. 3. K ०अरीणं, W ०त्वरीहिं. 4. K दोल्लदाहिँ, W भूखदाहिँ.

पडिट्ठाविदा[1]। सअं च दिक्खा [2]गहिदा। तदा ताए विण्णत्तो जोईसरो गुरुदक्खिणाणिमित्तं। भणिदं च तेण। जदि अवस्सं दक्खिणा दाअव्वा ता [3]एसा दीअदु। तदो देवीए विण्णत्तं जं आदिसदि [4]भअवं तं काअव्वं। पुण उल्लविदं-च तेण। अत्थि एत्थ लाडदेसम्मि चण्डसेणो णाम राआ। तस्स दुहिदा घणसारमञ्जरी-त्ति। सा [5]देवण्णएहिं आइट्ठा चक्कवट्टिघरिणी भविस्सदि-त्ति। तदो सा [6]महाराएण परिणाविदव्वा जेण गुरुस्स दक्खिणा दिण्णा भविस्सदि। भत्ता-वि चक्कवट्टि कदो होदि। तदो देवीए विहसिअ भणिदं जं आणवेदि भअवं तं कीरदि। अहं च विण्णविदुं पेसिदा। गुरुस्स गुरुदक्खिणा सा [8]दिण्णा।

विदूषकः। (विहस्य) ता उवक्खाणं एदं। ससिे सप्पो देसन्तरे वेज्जो। इह अज्ज विवाहो। लाडदेसे घणसारमञ्जरी।

राजा। किं [9]ते भइरवाणन्दस्स पहावो परोक्खो।

सारङ्गिका। देवीए कारिदे पमदुज्जाणस्स मज्झट्ठिदे वडतरुमूले चामुण्डाअदणे[10] भइरवाणन्दो [11]देवीए समं आगमिस्सादि। अग्गदो-अ दक्खिणाविहिदो केअईलदाहरए विवाहो भविस्सदि। ता इह ज्जेव देवेण गन्तव्वं। (इति परिक्रम्य निष्क्रान्ता)

राजा। (साकूतं) वअस्स [12]सव्वं एदं भइरवाणन्दस्स विअम्भिदं-ति तक्केमि।

---

1. K पड्डि०, W पदि०. 2. K गह्दिा, W. गदीहा. 3. K एसा दीअदु, W पसादीकयदु. 4. W *om.* 5. K देवस्रएहिं, W देवस्र एहिं. 6. K ०राएण, W ०रायह्त्थेण. 7. K तदो, W ता. 8. K दिण्णा W *om.* 9. N ते, K दे. 10. P आअदणे, W ०आययणे. 11. K देवीए समं, W देवी. 12. K सव्वं, W सच्चं.

विदूषकः । एवं णेदं । ण-हु मअलञ्छणमन्तरेण अण्णो मिअङ्कमणिपुत्तलिअं [1]पज्झरावेदि । ण-हु सरअसमीरमन्तरेण सेहालिआ कुसुमुक्करं वा किरेदि ।

(प्रविश्य) भैरवानन्दः । इअं सा वडतरुमूले णिक्कन्तस्स सुरङ्गादुवारस्स [2]पिधाणे चामुण्डा । (तां चामुण्डां हस्तेन प्रणम्य)

कप्पन्तकेलिभवणे कालस्स [3]असुराण रुहिरसुरपुरं ।
जअइ पिअन्ती काली परमेट्ठी-कवालचसएण ॥ १८ ॥

(प्रविश्योपविश्य च) अज्ज-वि ण णिग्गच्छदि सुरङ्गादुवारेण कप्पूरमञ्जरी ।

ततः प्रविशति सुरङ्गाद्वारोद्घाटननाटितकेन कर्पूरमञ्जरी ।

कर्पूरमञ्जरी । भअवं पणमिज्जसि ।

भैरवानन्दः । पुत्ति इच्छिअं वरं लह । इह जेव उपविस ।

कर्पूरमञ्जरी [4]उपविशति ।

भैरवानन्दः । (स्वगतम्) अज्ज-वि ण एदि देवी ।

प्रविश्य

राज्ञी । (परिक्रम्य पुरो विलोक्य च) अए इअं भअवदी चामुण्डा । (प्रणम्यावलोक्य च) अध इअं कप्पूरमञ्जरी । ता किं णेदं । (भैरवानन्दं प्रति) [5]इदं विण्णवीअदि णिअभवणे विवाहसामग्गिं कदुअ आगद-म्हि । तदो तं गेण्हिअ आगमिस्सं ।

भैरवानन्दः । वच्छे एवं कीरदु । राज्ञी व्यावृत्य परिक्रामति ।

---

1. K पञ्झरावेदि, W पञ्भवेदि. 2. K पिधाणे, W विधाणे. 3. W पुराण रु°. 4. K उपविशति, W तथा कृत्वा. 5. K इदं, W इयं.

भैरवानन्दः। (विहस्य स्वगतम्) इअं कप्पूरमञ्जरीघरं अण्णेसिदुं गदा[1]। (प्रकाशं) पुत्ति कप्पूरमञ्जरी सुरङ्गादुवारेण ज्जेव तुरिदपदं गदुअ णिअभवणे चिट्ठ। देवीए आगमणे पुणो [2]आगन्तव्वं। [3]कर्पूरमञ्जरी तथा करोति।

राज्ञी। इदं रक्खाघरं। (प्रविश्यावलोक्य च [4]स्वगतम्) अए इअं कप्पूरमञ्जरी। सा का-वि सारक्खिआ दिट्ठा। [5](प्रकाशं) वच्छे कप्पूरमञ्जरी कीदिसं ते सरीरं। (आकाशे) किं भणसि सिरे वेअणा [6]समुप्पण्ण-त्ति। ([7]स्वगतम्) ता पुणो गमिस्सं। (प्रविश्य पार्श्वाण्यवलोक्य) हला सहीओ विवाहोअरणाइ लहुं [8]गेण्हिअ आगच्छध। (इति परिक्रामति)

प्रविश्य कर्पूरमञ्जरी तथैवास्ते।

राज्ञी। (पुरोऽवलोक्य) इअं कप्पूरमञ्जरी।

भैरवानन्दः। वच्छे विब्भमलेहे आणीदाइं विवाहोवअरणाइं।

राज्ञी। अध इं। किं पुण घणसारमञ्जरीसमुचिदाइं आहरणाइं वीसरिआइं। ता पुणो गमिस्सं।

भैरवानन्दः। एवं भोदु। राज्ञी निष्क्रामति नाटितकेन।

भैरवानन्दः। कप्पूरमञ्जरि तं ज्जेव कीरदु।

कर्पूरमञ्जरी निष्क्रान्ता।

राज्ञी। (रक्षागृहप्रवेशं नाटयति। कर्पूरमञ्जरीं दृष्ट्वा) अए [9]सारिक्खएण विडम्बिदो-म्हि। (स्वगतं) झाणविमाणेण णिविग्घं

1. W *add.* इति निष्क्रान्ता. 2. K आगन्तव्वं, W आतेतव्वं.
3. K कर्पू॰...करोति, W कर्पू॰। जं भअवं आणवेदि। इति निष्क्रान्ता।
4. W *om.* 5. K प्रकाशं, W *om.* 6. W *om.* ॰त्ति. 7. W राज्ञी.
8. K गेण्हिअ, W गिण्हअ. 9. K सारिक्खदाए, W सिरिक्खएण,

परिसरे अप्पणो तं [1]आणेदि महाजोई। (प्रकाशं) जं जं णिवेदिदव्वं तं तं लहुअं गेण्हिअ आअच्छध। चामुण्डायतन-प्रवेशनाटितकेन तामवलोक्य) अहो सारक्खिदा।

भैरवानन्दः। देवि उववित्ससु। महाराओ आगदो ज्जेव वट्टदि।

ततः प्रविशति राजा विदूषकः कुरङ्गिका च।

भैरवानन्दः। आसणं महाराअस्स।

सर्वे यथोचितमुपविशन्ति।

राजा। (जनान्तिकम् [?]) एसा सा कप्पूरमञ्जरी। [2]सरीरिणी [3]मअरध्वअपारिद्धिआ देहन्तरसंठिदसिङ्गारसवरचावलट्ठी दिवस-सञ्चारिणी पुण्णिमाइन्दुचन्दिआ। अवि-अ गुणगणमाणिक्क-सुत्तिआ [4]रअणमई अञ्जणसलाआ। जधा-अ एसा [5]आरण्णकुसुम-णिप्फण्णा महुलच्छी। किं-च

भुवणजअपडीआ रूअरेहा इमीए
जह तह णअणाणं गोअरं जस्स जादि।
वसइ [6]मअरकेऊ तस्स चित्ते विचित्ते
वलइअधणुदण्डो पुङ्खिदेहिं सरेहिं॥ १९॥

विदूषकः। (जनान्तिकम्) सच्चं कदं तए आहाणअं। [7]तडं

---

1. K आणेदि, W तमाणेदि. 2. K सरीरिणी, W कर्पूरमञ्जरी सारक्खिदा विलासचरणी, 3. W °रद्धियपरिद्धिआ. 4. K रअणमई. W मणिजअणमअस्स. 5. O अरण्णकुसुमणिप्फण्णा, W लावण्णकुसुमणिसण्णा. 6. K मअरकेऊ, W मयरद्धो. 7. K तडं W महाणयतडं.

गदाए वि णावाए ण विस्ससीअदि । [1]ता तुण्हीओ चिट्ठ ।

भैरवानन्दः । वच्छे पत्तं विवाहमङ्गलमुहुत्तं । ता महाराअस्स किज्जदु तए जधोचिदप्पडिवण्णं ।

राज्ञी । कुरङ्गिए तुमं महाराअस्स विवाहणेवच्छं कुरु । सारङ्गिआ-वि घणसारमञ्जरीए करेदु ।

इत्युभे अप्युभयोर्विवाहघटनां नाटयतः ।

भैरवानन्दः । वच्छे उवज्झाओ हक्कारीअदु ।

राज्ञी । [2]एसो वि उंवज्झाओ अज्जकविञ्जलो चिट्ठदि । ता कीरदु अग्गिआरिअं ।

विदूषकः । भो वअस्स उत्तरीए गण्ठिं दाइस्सं दाव । परिणेदु महाराओ कप्पूरमञ्जरी । (इति हस्ते हस्तं ग्राहयति कर्पूरमञ्जर्याः)

[3]राज्ञी । (स्वगतं) किं णेदं ।

भैरवानन्दः । उवज्झाओ सुट्ठुदरं भुल्लो-सि । जदो कप्पूर-मञ्जरीए [4]घणसारमञ्जरि-त्ति णामन्तरं ।

राजा । (करमादाय)

जे [5]कण्टआ तिउसमुद्धफलेसु होन्ति
जे केअईकुसुमगन्धदलावलीसु ।
फंसेण [6]णूणमिह मज्झ सरीरतुल्ला
ते सुन्दरीए बहलं पुलअंकुरिल्ला ॥ ३० ॥

---

1. K तुण्हीओ चिट्ठ, *for* W *see* Note. 2. W *add* अज्जउत्त *before* एसो. 3. W राज्ञी इत्याकर्ण्य...णेदं इति चमत्कृत्य. 4. W *has* अपरं *after* त्ति. 5. K कण्टआ, W के वित्ते. 6. O °मिह, K तुह.

विदूषकः। भो वअस्स भामरीओ दिज्जन्तु। हुअवहे लाजा खिपिज्जन्तु।

भ्रामर्यो नाटयन्ति नायका [:]। धूमेन व्यावृत्तमुखी
राज्ञी सपरिवारा निष्क्रान्ता[1]।

चतुर्थं जवनिकान्तरम्।

---

1. W *add.* सव्वाणं पच्चक्खं परिणीदा कप्पूरमञ्जरी *and the* Southern mss. *add the following :*

नेपथ्ये

वैतालिकः। सुहाअ भोदु विवाहमहूसवो देवस्स।

जं मूद्धं तिमिसं णवं च पणसं जे पारिभद्ददुमा
जे दण्डा कमलाण किं च कुसुमं जं केअईसंभवं।
सव्वे तुज्झ कलेवरे गुणगणं लद्धं बला तारिसा
रोमञ्चा फुडपुट्ठकण्टअमिसा मेल्लन्ति णिव्वुल्लसा॥

भैरवानन्दः। अण्णं किं दे पिअं करीअदु।

राजा। इदो वि परं किं पिअं। जदो
देवी रोसकसाअमाणसवई णो होइ सावत्तए
लद्धा पुण्णससङ्कमण्डलमुही सिङ्गाररसञ्जीविणी।
सञ्जाआ अवि चक्कवट्टिपअवी किं अण्णमब्भत्थणं
सव्वं तुज्झ अणुग्गहेण भरिअं जं माणुसे लब्भइ॥

तधा वि इदं भोदु।

भरतवाक्यम्

अणुदिअहं विफुरन्तो मणीसिजणसअलगुणविणासअरो।
रित्तत्तणदावग्गी विरमउ कमलाकडक्खवरिसेण॥

इति निष्क्रान्ताः सर्वे।

KARPŪRAMAÑJARĪ

Notes : Critical and Exegetical*

ACT. I

P. 1. l. 1. s a r a s s a i e (=*sarasvatyai*). The Skt. word *bhadra* (=Pkt *bhadda*) requires the dative case. See Pāṇini, II. 3. 73. Hence we have preferred *sarassaīe* to *sarassia. Kaiṇo* (=*kaveḥ*) should be taken with *sarassaīe*, and the meaning of the whole expression will be, 'May the speech of the poet flourish.' Cf. *gumpho vāṇīnāṃ vijayate*, Bālar. I. 1., *bhāratī kaver jayati*, Kāvyaprakāśa I. 1. Others including old commentators construe *kaiṇo* with *vāsūiṇo* and in that case the expression will mean 'May the goddess S. flourish.' But such a meaning is improper, for no one need bless a goddess. Vāsudeva's defence of this construction is unsatisfactory.

l. 2. a ṇ ṇ ā ṇ a ṃ-p i—'of others too' i.e., of the lesser poets, such as the author of the play ; cf. Lanman, p. 223, n3.

p a a ṭ ṭ d u. Southern mss. read *pavaṭṭadu* but as they read *ppaaṭṭa* and *pauṭṭa* in i. 4^{2} and i. 4^{16} respectively, in this case we have followed the Northern mss.

l. 3. k i ṃ-p i—an adverb to *phuradu*. It means 'to some extent'. The reading *kiṃ-ca* (=moreover, and again, further) occurring in other mss. seems to impoverish the sense. In this work Rāj. has principally used

---

* Reference to individual words and expressions within these Notes refer (unless otherwise mentioned) to the Harvard edition of the KM,

two rītis : Vaidarbhī and Māgadhī (=Gauḍī) with occasional sprinkling of Pāñcālī. Hence he says, 'May Vaidarbhī and Māgadhī styles occur to us and the Pāñcālikā as well, to some extent.'

phuradu (=*sphuratu*)—'start into view', 'become manifest', 'appear clearly,' 'become displayed.'

l. 4. rīdiā olihantu (=*rītīḥ avalihantu*) 'let (them) taste the rītis'. '*o-lih* (=*ava-lih*)' means 'to taste'; cf. *avalehiā* (= *avalehikā*) a kind of sweet thick paste (see Pāiasaddamahaṇṇavo, *sub voce*). Mss. and K. have divided the members of the expression as *rīāo* (*rīdīāo*) *lihantu* (let them lick the rītis) much to the impoverishment of the sense.

l. 5. dūram—'entirely,' 'completely'; cf. *dūram uddhūtapāpāḥ*, Meghadūta I, 55. It is an adv. to the three adjs. of *mohaṇāiṃ* and not to *ṇamaha* as has been taken by Lanman.

l. 6. ghaṇatāḍaṇāiṃ. The word *ghaṇa* means here 'violent' or 'coarse' (cf. the sense of *sthūla* in the *sthūlahastāvalepān*, Meghadūta. I. 14). On this point see Vātsyāyana, ch. vi (Sāmprayogikādhikaraṇa). The reading *thaṇatāḍaṇāiṃ* would impoverish the sense, for *tāḍaṇa* according to the Kāmaśāstra relates not only to *thaṇa* (breast) but to other parts of the body as well.

l. 7. (nāndyante) sūtradhāraḥ. The substitution of *sthāpaka* in late mss. seems to be due to a misunderstanding of I. 12^{1-3}. which stands very corrupt there. See Introduction § 35.

l. 8. sammohaṇāsāṇam. 'The destoyer of ignorance'. On harms proceeding from *sammoha* see the Bhagavadgītā, II, 62. The reading *chammuha* (=*ṣaṇmukha*) creates difficulty, for it is not easy to explain why of the two sons of Śiva and Pārvatī, only Kārttikeya should be given preference. Cf. Lanman. Vāsudeva reads *samoha-ṇāsāṇa** and explains it variously.

l. 9. d e u . Śaurasenī, it is believed, requires *dedu*. In fact mss. NODG going back probably to one archetype read it as such. This may however be a later emendation, for in some cases *all* mss. read similar forms, e. g., *bolei* (II. 29^{d}), *dei* (II. 37^{b}), *lihaï* (II. 40^{b}), *paāsaï* (III. 11^{d}), *paaḍei* (III. 12^{c}, 17^{d}). For a discussion on such cases see Introduction § 22.

l. 11. j a l e ṇ a ṃ. The plural in *jalehiṃ* seems to encumber the sense unduly ; cf. II. 30^{b}.

l. 12. -s i p p ī a. It is equivalent to Skt. **sīpyā*, instr. of **sīppī*. Ś. being nearer to Skt. than any other Pkt. this reading has been adopted against *sippīe* in W. For the Ś. character of the metrical passages see Introduction (§§ 21,22). *Sippī* is both a small boat-shaped vessel used in *pūjā* for offering water, and a bivalve shell, which may be extended to mean conch-shell. The word occurs in NIA.

P. 2. l. 1. k i ṃ-p u ṇ a. The reading *kiṃ-uṇa* seems to be wrong ; see Pischel, Grammatik § 143. Similar want of voicing of the initial unvoiced stop of the next word is to be met with in *kiṃ-ca* (I. 1^{c} .), *tihuaṇaṃ-pi* (I. 10^{a}). Woolner seems to follow Sten Konow ; see 'Introduction to Pkt.' ch. iv. § 3.

l. 2. p a v a ñ c a (=*prapañca*).—'group', 'crowd' etc.

l. 3. i a r ā. Konow reads *idarā* without support from any mss.

l. 4. p a ṭ ṭ a c...v a ṭ ṭ e d i—'pounding on a slab of stone'. This expression is an exact equivalent of New Bengali *pāṭāy bāṭe* পাটায় বাটে.

l. 5. ṭ h ā v i d o ṭ h ā ṇ e (=*sthāpitaḥ sthāne*). *lit.* has been placed in tone (*sthāna*).

P. 2. l. 6. t i ṇ ṇ i-v i m i a ṅ g ā. *Tiṇṇi* (= *trīṇi*) is used in all genders and is an example of the confusion of gender in Pkt. (see Pischel, Grammatik § 438); *tiṇṇi* is the source of NIA *tin* তিন, *tīn* तीन, etc.

e s a......h a l a v o l o. Here the reading of the best mss. W and B is wrong; for in it *tāla* (cymbal), an important instrument of the musical orchestra, has been omitted, while *pakkhāujja* (Hindī *pakhāwaj* पखावज) which is the same thing as the *miaṅga* (= *mṛdaṅga*) has been needlessly brought in a second time.

l. 7. p a k k h ā l a ṇ u j j ā l a ṇ a means 'cleansing' (= *prakṣālana*) and 'polishing' (*ujjālaṇa*). The care taken about the polishing of cymbals evidently gives a clue to the position of the orchestra in the stage.

e v a ṃ—'in this manner.' This use of the word probably gave rise to New Bengali এবং as a copulative conj. meaning 'and'.

d h u v ā g ī d a ṃ (= *dhruvāgītam*). Lanman has missed the sense of this. Dhruvā songs are to be sung on particular occasions in course of producing a play. For rules regarding the use of such songs which should always be in Ś. see NŚ. ch. xxxii. Examples of such songs given in this work (NŚ.) have been edited by the present writer in IHQ, vol. viii. 1932. The word *dhuvā* gives New Bengali *dhuā* ধুআ, ধুয়া burden of a song.

l. 8. k u ḍ u m b a ṃ (= *kuṭumbam*). This should better be translated as 'a member of the family' or 'of the party of actors' and not as an 'attendant' as Lanman does.

h a k k ā r i a.—'calling'. This verb has its equivalent in New Bengali *hā kār deoā* হাঁকার দেওয়া, to call from a distance.

l. 14. k o-u ṇ a (=*kaḥ-punaḥ*). This seems to give Hindī *kaün* कौन, Bengali *kon* কোন্, etc.

l. 16. b h a ṇ ṇ a i. The usual Śauraseni form would be *bhaṇṇadi* (=*bhaṇyate*) which no ms. gives. The form *bhaṇijjadi* spoils the metre. The developed form of this word is due to its being the part of a stereotyped living expression. In Early Maithili *bhaṇaï Vidyāpati bhāṇe* (=*bhaṇati Vidyāpatir* [*etad*] *bhaṇyate* [*ca*]) we have *bhaṇṇaï* >*bhāṇe*.

P. 3. l. 4. d ū r a ṃ. See *dūraṃ* explained above.

n ā ḍ i ā e (=*nāṭikāyāḥ*). In Skt. the root *anu-kṛ* (=to imitate) is used with the genitive or the accusative; see V. S. Apte, Guide to Skt. § 118.

l. 5. p a v e s a-v i k k h a m b h a ā i......ṇ a t t h i (=*praveśa-viṣkambhakādi*.........*nāsti*).

l. 6. p ā i a b a n d ° e p a a ṭ ṭ o k a ī. *Pāia* instead of *pāüa*, is correct, because *ṛ* < *u* seems to be no Ś. characteristic. See the description of Ś. as given in the NŚ. ch. xviii (xvii) and the editor's paper 'Date of the Bharata-Nāṭyaśāstra' (Journal of the Dept. of Letters, Calcutta Univ. XXV. 1934) All mss. except ABPW, give after this passage the following :

parusā sakkaa-bandhā pāua-bandho-vi hoi suumāro
purisa-mahilāṇaṃ jettiam ihantaraṃ tettiam imāṇaṃ.

This stanza does not occur in the best ms. W, and a very old ms. B., and modifies the statement about the practical similarity between Pkt. and Skt. (one being the evolution of the other) and the author's indifference about the language to be employed in a kāvya, which is immediately to follow. Hence it has been considered spurious.

l. 8. s a b b a b h ā s ā-c a d u r e ṇ a etc. In all

P. 3. mss. except BWAP. this sentence has been preceded by *parusā* etc. See Note on l. 6 above.

l. 9. **a t t h a v i s e s ā** (=*arthaviśeṣāḥ*). *Visesā* here means 'excellences' and the whole stanza may be paraphrased as follows : The same is the excellence of meaning, and words are also the same (in Pkt. as well as in Skt.) the former being the modification (of the latter. Moreover it is) excellent expressions (that constitute) a poem, be the language whatever it may.

l. 9. **t e c c i a, t e c c e v a.** *Ccia* and *cceva* seem to have come from the Skt. phrase *tac caiva.* From *tacceva* we have *taccia* ; *cceva* (*ccia*) • wrongly separated from the phrase stands as a substitute of Skt. *eva*.

l. 10. **j ā h o u s ā h o u.** This MIA expression has its exact equivalent in New Bengali *jā hok tā hok* যা হোক্ তা হোক (= in any manner).

l. 11. **t ā a p p ā k i ṃ-ṇ a v a ṇ ṇ i d o t e ṇ a** etc. The way of eulogising oneself by quoting an admirer seems to be an original device of Rāj.

l. 12. **s u ṇ a d u.** This reading occurring in the best ms. W, is the proper reading, for nominative in the third person makes the verb honorific while Konow's *suṇasu* puts the verb in the second person which is used among intimate relations.

l. 14. **u v a j j h ā o** (= *upâdhyāyaḥ*) gives the NIA *ojhā* ওঝা, ओझा, *jhā* झा.

l. 13. **A v a r ā i a.** 'Āparājiti' occurring in the Kāvyamīmāṃsā (p. 45) may be an adj. from this name.

P. 4. l. 3. **C ā h u ā ṇ a k u l a-m a ü l i m ā l i ā** etc.— This is indeed a novel occasion for the production of plays which are usually staged in days of religious and other festivals (see the Abhinayadarpaṇa, 13-14). About the importance of this play in settling the chronology of Rāj.'s plays see Introduction § 32.

l. 8. s a m p ā ḍ e m h a. The root *pāḍ* is the causative form of *paḍ* (= *paṭ*).

j a d o.........c i ṭ ṭ h a d i. This sentence has been very badly handed down and stands more or less mutilated in all the mss. For a full discussion on its reconstruction see Introduction § 25.

l. 14. ṇ a n d a ṇ e. The Skt. form is *nandini*. All mss. except WO. have the Sanskritised form in *ṇandiṇi*.

v a d d h ā v i a s i. This word is cognate with Hindī, *badhāvā*, बधावा 'festive' joy and Middle Bengali *bādhāi* বাধাই as in *ānanda-bādhāi* আনন্দবাধাই (cf. Skt. *vardhāpana*). The alternative reading *vaḍḍhāvīasi* is however cognate with the NIA root *būḍh* (to increase, to grow) which also is from the Skt. root *vṛdh*.

l. 16. m a a ṇ a. This word is equivalent to Skt. **mṛdana* or **mradana* (softening). Hence *maaṇa* relates to anything oily or fatty like bee's wax or butter, and not to wax alone. Bengali word *mayān* ময়ান meaning 'ghee used with flour to be made into *lucis* লুচি or fried wafers to make them tender in the mouth, is connected with this word.

P. 5. l. 3. p a ḍ i v a d d h ā v i ā. See the Note on *vaddhāvīasi* above.

l. 4. c h o l l a n t i. *Cholla* a means to 'cleanse'; cf. NIA. *chol* to cleanse, to scrape.

l. 6. s u v a n t i (= *svapanti*). This Pkt. root *suva* is responsible for the NIA root *so* (= *śo* শো) meaning 'to sleep', 'to lie down'.

l. 7. p e c c h a (= *prekṣa*). For the place of the development *kṣ* > *ch* in Ś. see Introduction § 17b.

ll. 8ff. j a a p u v v a d i g a ṅ g a ṇ ā b h u a ṅ g a

P. 5. etc. This passage has suffered much in transmission. See Notes on different words below.

b h u a ṅ g a —'gallant, lover, husband or lord in general'. In all the five adjs. the countries have been considered as a *nāyikā* to the king.

C a m p ā-c a m p a a-k a ṇ ṇ a ū r a. Very dear (*lit. c.* ear-ornament) to the land named Campā (modern Bhagalpur).

R ā ḍ h ā j a ṇ i d a r ā ḍ h a. 'One who has caused lustre (prosperity) to the country named Rāḍhā' (the modern Burdwan dist. of Bengal, and some adjoining places).

C a ṅ g a t t a ṇ a ṇ i j j i d a-k ā m a r ū v a. Konow has unneccessarily disregarded the testimoney of his best ms. and tagged *caṅgattaṇa* to the previous adj. but it fitly goes along with *Kāmarūva* (= *Kāmarūpa* in Assam). The word *caṅgattaṇa* has two meanings : (i) beauty, (ii) strength, and so has *Kāmarūva* : (i) one having a power to assume any form (even the most beautiful one) according to one's desire. (ii) the name of a country. In Konow's reading the pun has been spoiled.

H a r i k e l i-k e l i ā r a—The provider of sports to Harikelī (Bengal of the delta).

l. 10. a v a m a ṇ ṇ i d a-K a ṇ ṇ a s u v a ṇ ṇ a-d ā ṇ a. One who has disregarded the bribe or payment of the people of Karṇasuvarṇa (modern Murshidabad district) against the invasion of their territory. The reading *jaccasuvaṇṇa* though it stands in the best mss. may be disregarded ; for Karṇasuvarṇa is a well-known geographical name signifying an Eastern country like Rāḍhā, Kārmarūpa etc., and as such it embellishes the expression. Surely the king has been eulogised here as the lord of Eastern countries like Rāḍhā, Kāmarūpa etc.

Karṇasuvarṇa has lately been located in the the Northern Rāḍhā (R. Basak. 'The Hist. of North-Eastern India, Calcutta, 1934, p. 132.)

l 11. i h a. The Ś. form *idha* occuring in Pkt. grammar of Hemacandra (iv. 268) does not seem to occur in Pkt. literature (see Pāiasaddamahaṇṇava *sub voce*). The mss. of KM. too except one, read *iha*, and see NŚ. (Chaukhamba ed.) on Ś. It gives a rule that except in case of *yathā* and *tathā*, *th* of Skt. will be *h* in Ś (ch. xviii. 15). See M. Ghosh, 'Date of the Bharata NŚ.'

l. 13. C o ḍ a-c o ḍ â l a ā ṇ a ṃ. The bodice and hairs of the Cola women. The word *cola* (Skt.) meaning 'inhabitant of Cola' as well as a 'bodice' goes back to Pkt. *coḍa*.

l. 17. r a m a ṇ ī g a ṇ ḍ a p p a h a. The reading *Maraḍhī* does not occur in the best mss. and it is not necessary; *kuṃkuma* when applied to women's face is said to make it as fair as full moon's face (see Lanman, in p. 226 note 6). Besides this, there is no literary or other tradition making Marāṭhī women fairer than their sisters in other parts of India.

P. 6. l. 5. k a n d a l i d a-k a n d a p p a-k o d a ṇ ḍ a-c a ṇ ḍ i m a. *Kandalida* means 'fighting'; cf. Skt. *kandala* 'battle'. *Daṇḍa* means 'assault'. The whole expression in translation will be 'that which is terrible on account of the assault that may proceed from the bow of Kandarpa (Cupid) who is in a fighting mood'. Cf. Lanman.

l. 6. ṇ i d d h a b a n d h a v a ṃ, Mss. other than WBA read *siṇiddha* and this from also may be allowed. See Vararuci, iii. 64.

v i t t h ā r i d a............p e c c h a. Konow reads *pekkha* against *peccha* in majority of mss. including the best one. See Introduction § 17b. As for widening the

P, 6. eyes for enjoying a pleasing sight cf. *Bharatâvalokanârtham viśālīkriyatām te cakṣuḥ*, Bhāsa's Pratimā, Acts iv and vii.

l. 7. m a h o c c h a v a ṃ. The great festival (i. e. of the spring) which is being celebrated by the dance of maidens and creepers, and songs of cuckoos. cf. *vasantūsao* in I. 13 above, Mss. other than BPW have either *mahūsava* or *mahussava.*

l. 15. d i ṭ ṭ h a m. means 'look'. The reading *diṭṭhiṃ* of K is unnecessary. Cf. Skt. *kṛtam, śrutam* etc.

P. 7. l. 1. t u m h ā ṇ a ṃ s a v v a s ṣ i ṃ. *Savva* (= *sarva*) in this expression with its inherent plural idea dispensed with the plural form. The use of two different case-endings in the same sense seems be due to a blending of two expressions *tumhāṇaṃ majjhe* and *savvassiṃ majjhe*, such a state of affairs being expected naturally in Pkt. which was the language of the common people.

k ā la k k h a r i a (= kālâkṣarika)—lit. one who has learnt how to write letters witk black ink. In the system of primary education as current even now in India, the child has to learn writing his letters and write them first with chalk and then with ink.

l. 2. j a s s a s a s u r o p a r a g h a r e s u p o t t h i ā i v a h a n t a o ā s ī. In this sentence interpolators have tried their hands, much to the detriment of the sense, *Sasuro* in enough to create humour. *Potthiāi* is enquivalent to Skt. *pusktaādi* i. e. 'books and other things' and this 'other things' makes a sly hint about water and fire-wood (which a domestic servant has to carry). This deepens the humour. The reading *potthiaiṃ* (= *pustakāṇi* or books) ignores this and damages the sense very much.

l, 3. k a m ā g a d a ṃ (= kramâgatam),—'coming in succession'.

l. 6. b h a m a r a ṭ e ṇ ṭ ā—*teṇṭā* is a *deśī* word meaning 'the gambling hall'; the expression is not very clear and may mean 'one whose passion takes her constantly from one man to another (lit. bee in a gambling hall). Cf. Lanman.

t e ṇ ṭ ā k a r ā l ā—In a Pkt. compound, members are sometimes transposed; *ṭeṇṭā* in this expression is same as the the word in the previous expression. Here the expression means 'one who is a terror of of the the gambling hall'. Cf. Beng. *juācor* জুয়াচোর cheat (lit. a thief of a gambler).

l. 7. t u ṭ̊ ṭ h a s a ṅ g h a ḍ i d e—one who provides satisfaction to others (by her person). After uttering this word the angry Vidūṣaka abruptly stops abusing Vicakṣaṇā whom he now challenges in a literary duel. A group of mss. or rather their original has wrongly added something to complete the unutterd sentence.

h a t t h e k a ṅ k a ṇ e k i ṃ d a p p a ṇ e ṇ a—Konow reads *paramparā-paṇḍiccassa......paramparāe paṇḍiccaṃ* before this. But the best ms. and several others do not contain this. We find it quite unnecessary. Old type of *kaṅkaṇas* (bangles or wrist-bands) had small mirrors fixed on them. Thus, one having a bangle had no need of a mirror. The expression in hand is, as has been guessed by Lanman, a proverb. It is often met with in NIA language and literature. Its modern counterpart in Hindī is '*hāth-kaṅgan-ko ārsī kyā*, हाथ कङ्गनको आरसी क्या; cf. also Old Bengali *hāthe re kāṅkāṇa mā loü dāpaṇa* হাথে রে কাঙ্কাণ মা লোউ দাপণ (= *haste re kaṅkaṇaḥ mā lokatu darpaṇam*) 'O you have a kaṅkaṇa in hand, do not look for a mirror, '*Rāma-ko rūpa nihārati Jānakī kaṅgaṇa-ke naga-ke parachāhi* रामको रूप निहारति

जानकी कङ्कणके नगके पदकाहि Rasika-vihārī. Lanman's explanation of this expression is however different. (see p. 225)

a h a. See notes on *iha* (p. 71)

l. 8. t u r a ṅ g a s s a—Konow reads *dhāvantassa* as an adj. to this word but most of the mss. including the best one have no support for him. The meaning also does not suffer without this addition. For *turaṅga*, is used here in its etymological sense and means 'a swift horse' and to ascertain the swiftness of such an animal one must ride it or see it ridden and not ask for the testimony of others. This also seems to be a proverbial expression like, 'The test of the pudding is in the eating.'

p i a v a a s s a s s a d e v ī e p u r a d o—Vidūṣaka wants to recite before the queen, just as Vicakṣaṇā is asked by the queen to recite before the king (*ajjaiūttassa purado*, I, 19[6]). Here the reading of the best mss. seems to be wrong.

l. 18. k a n t ā-r a t t a ṇ a—*rattaṇa* means *rañjana* ; the root *rattaya* being a *nāmadhātu* from *ratta* (= *rakta*).

P. 8. l. 3. t u v a ṃ—This form is very old and is met with in Aśvaghoṣa (see Keith. Skt. Drama, p. 88)

l. 5. n i v v a h a d i—lit. this means 'carries' i. e., 'supports the genuineness of'. Cf. the Skt. root, *nir-vaha*, means 'to support'.

l. 12. s a c c a ṃ v i a k k h a ṇ ā.............. u t t ī ṇ a ṃ—This passage has suffered much in transmission. N. gives the true reading. The passage in translation will be 'Truely V. is an expert in clever sayings, (lit. in the cleverness of sayings).

l. 13. t ā k i ṃ p i a ṇ ṇ a ṃ v i c i t t a d ā e —This passage too has not been properly preserved. B. here seems to give the correct reading. P. also may be said to support this. In the reading of W., *a* and *cadura*-

vaaṇa is superfluous, for we have *cadurattaṇa* of *utti* in the previous sentence. What the king means to say here is that 'as her power of composing clever things has been demonstrated, what is the use of demanding in her case brilliance (*vicittadā*) of other kinds i. e. of rīti (style) or of alaṃkāra (figures of speech)' ? In this passage Rāj. shows himself as a critic of high order. This sentence is followed in W. by the following *kiṃ bhannai sukaï cūḷāmaṇe ṭhidāe esā. Devi ajja kiṃ edaṃ mahīyalasarassaï esā Viakkhaṇā eva. Devī* (*vihasya*) *kavicūḍāmaṇittaṇeṇa ṭhidā esā.* This part is evidently corrupt and possibly due to some interpolation.

l. 16. a c c ā d h a m a (= *atyadhama*). The lengthening of the second *a* is due to the analogy of expressions like *narādhama*, *adhamādhama*, *atyāhita* etc. The reading *accadhama* is due to Skt. influence.

b a m b h a ṇ o—This reading (and not *bamhaṇo*) is evidently the older and the right reading, for it retains the fuller form of the word (see Keith, Skt. Drama, p. 86).

P. 9. l. 1. t u ṇ ḍ i l ā e v i a k a ñ c u l i ā—In Pkt. *tuṇḍilā* seems to be preferable to *tundilā* which seems to be its Sanskritised form ; *kañculiā* has its NIA form *kā̃culi*.

l. 3. t u b b h a—This is evidently a much older form than *tujjha* <**tuhya* <*tubhya* ; *cf. mahya* <**mabhya* which is comparable to Avestic *māvōya*.

l. 4. p a ḍ i p a ṭ ṭ e v i a ṭ a s a r i v i r a a ṇ ā—*Paḍipaṭṭa* (= *pratipaṭṭa*) the reverse of wearing apparel i.e. the side which is not open to view ; *ṭasariviraaṇā* means 'embroidery made with *ṭasara*' (Skt. *tasara*) a kind of cream-coloured silk.

l. 6. t u v a ṃ—see before.

v a ṇ ṇ i a s i—'are praised', the root *varṇ*=to praise.

l, 8. ṇ ā r ā o v i a ṇ i r k k h a r o—'as unlettered as a jewellers' weighing apparatus' in which are used small guñjās or stones and no weight-pieces marked with letters such as 1 seer, 2 seers etc. (see also below ; cf. Hāla's Gāthā-saptaśatī, II, 91).

l. 9. t u l l a - v v a l a d d h a k k h a r ā,—'one who has got letters like a big weighing machine' which uses big pieces of stone marked with figures such as 1, 2, 3, etc., indicating seers and maunds etc.

l. 11. J u h i ṭ ṭ h i l a. This form of the word with *l* instead of *r* shows the Eastern affinity of Vidūṣaka's language which according to the NŚ. is the Prācyā an (Eastern) variety of Ś. Cf. Pāli *yudhiṭṭhila*.

l. 13. t a ḍ a t t i. (=*taḍat*+*iti*) 'as swift as lightning' (*taḍat*=*taḍit*).

P. 10. l. 6. s ā ḍ o l i ā. This seems to be a genuine *deśī* word though K. ignores it. This word is probably cognate with Bengali শাড়ী and Skt. *śāṭī*. Konow, however, reads *sāhuliā* against the testimony of the best ms.

l. 8. r ā ü l a s s a—Konow reads *rāaülassa*. Vr. allows both the forms (see iv. 1.) but as the best ms. gives *rāüla* we have adopted this.

l. 10. k ī r a d i (=*kriyate*) Pischel denies that it is a Ś. word and finds fault with Indian editors (see Grammatik § 547). The long *ī* of *kīra* is probably due to analogy of *dīsadi*, *suṇīadi*, *curīadu*, etc.

l. 12. j a ṃ...b h a a v a ṃ s a m u v v a h a d i. Śiva wears *ardhacandra* on his forehead. Now the 'ardhacandra' gesture by hand indicates among other things 'turning one by one's neck' (*gala-hasta-dāna*). Lanman's interpretation of the passage is not clear and he misunderstands the meaning of the 'ardhacandra' hand (see IHQ. XII. 1936, p. 736).

l. 16. m a h a b a m b h a ṇ a s s a (= *mahābrāhmaṇasya*) 'of a mahā-brāhmaṇa'. M. is a Brāhman who has degraded himself by accepting gifts given at the first śrāddha offered to the dead *i.e.* an *agraśrāddhahāraka*, Dr. A. K. Ryder has made a very unfortunate blunder over this latter term. See JAOS, Vol. 23, p. 79. Vidūṣaka's reference to himself as a Mahābrāhmaṇa is meant for creating fun. This device has been used by dramatists like Kālidāsa, Śrīharṣa etc. The adj. *mahat* when compounded with *śaṅkha*, *taila*, *māṃsa*, *vaidya*, *jyotiṣin* and *dvija* (*brāhmaṇa*) degrades, their sense. *Mahābrahma* in Bhaṭṭi-kāvya (1. 4) may be called an exception to this rule or it may be justified in a different manner.

P. 11 l. 8. ṇ i a v a s u n d h a r ā ṇ ā m a - b a m b h a ṇ ī e. The confusion of word-order in this compound is in keeping with the genius of Pkt. Vidūṣaka's feigned agitated state may also be responsible for this.

l. 17. *sohañjaṇa*. This is the Pkt. form of the Skt. *śobhāñjana*, In Hindī it is *sahijana* सहिजन and in Bengali *sājinā* সাজিনা. *Sājinā* flowers are sometimes cooked and eaten and hence a *sohañjaṇa* tree is often made flowerless and this treatment of the tree by people occurs in the month of Phālguna. The Vidūṣaka curses Vicakṣāṇa by saying that she may be flowerless (*niṣpuṣpā*) which for a woman means becoming old.

l. 15. l a m b a k u c c a ṃ ... k ī r d u. 'Give her mask with long beards and ears as big as tappara and let her occupy my place for creating laughter'. Vidūṣaka says that though they (*i.e.* the king and the queen) have praised Vicakṣaṇā more than himself yet she cannot replace him. But by wearing a laughable mask she may make an attempt to do so. Ṭappara is a big hat-like thing which rural people wear on their head for protection against the sun. The word is probably connected with Bengali *ṭopar* টোপর, a kind of headgear used (mostly) on cermonial occasions = Middle Bengali 'helmet'.

l. 16. m u d a (= mṛta). Cf. Hindī *mūā*, मुआ.

ll. 2-3. a ṇ u ṇ a a k a k k a s o......g ā ḍ h a d a r o b h o d i, 'This Brahman Kapiñjala is (liable to be) made harsh by entreaties; (for) hempen rope when soaked in water becomes tighter'.

P. 12. l. 12, B h a i r a v â ṇ a n d a d u v ā r e. 'Bh. is at the door. This is one complete sentence, and another is *uvavissadi* 'he will sit.' Konow probably connects this to the preceding expression in one sentence and finds the mss. wrong on this point. Hence his reading is *Bh. duvāre ciṭṭhadi.*

l. 13. a c c a b b h u a (= *atyadbhuta*). cf. Bengali *ācābhūā* আচাভুয়া strange.

P. 13. l. 3. m a n t o ṇ a t a n to ṇ a etc. For the true explanation of this stanza and two following ones see Introduction § 27. Cf. *ekka ṇa kijjai manta ṇa tanta, nia gharaṇi laï keli karanta/niaghara-ghariṇi jāva ṇa majjaï, tāva ki pañcavarṇa (ṇṇa ?) viharijjaï*—28—Kṛṣṇācārya-pāda's Dohā (বৌদ্ধ গান ও দোঁহা H. P. Shastri's ed.).

P. 15. l. 4. c i t t e l i h i j j a d i ṇ a k a s s a. 'In whose heart is she not to be impressed' (lit. be inscribed). To Lanman *citta* is equivalent to Skt. *citra*, 'picture.

l. 8. o l l a ṃ s u - u l l ā s i - t h a ṇ u l l a ṇ ā e (= *ārdrāṃsukollāsistanolvaṇāyāḥ*). **Ulvaṇā* means *ulvaṇatvaṃ* 'manifestness'. Hence the whole expression means 'of one whose breasts have been disclosed by wet clothes'. This expression has been much damaged in transmission. The best ms. too stands distorted. B.

gives the clue to the true reading. Its reading *ghaṇul-laṇā* seems to be due to a confusion between Devanāgarī *tha* थ and *dha* ध.

P. 16. l. 1. r ū v a s o h ā. The beauty of form (rūpa = physical form); cf. *gorūpadharām ivorvīm*, Raghu. II. 3.

l. 6. k a d h a m ...... a h a v ā. This sentence and the following verse have been attributed by a group of mss. including W. to the jester. But from the context this appears to be wrong. BPNOR here correctly read the passage as a continuation of the king's speech.

l. 8. r ū v e ṇ a m u k k ā o etc. In this case too the best ms. is misleading. The stanza in translation will be as follows: 'Those who are without (beautiful) form (of their body) can be given beauty by ornaments; (for) their charm is dependent on ornaments, but the charm of persons who are naturally possessed of beauty is not enhanced by ornaments.' The king means to say that Karpūramañjarī is naturally beautiful and hence her beauty is not dependent on ornaments. The corruption of this stanza has probably been effected by the speech of Vidūṣaka in Act II. 25 where using partly a similar language he gives a diametrically opposite view which does not rise above the commonplace while the king's words bespeak a very refined taste.

l. 15. j ā ṇ e ... s o ṇ ḍ ī r a t t a ṇ a m. This passage has suffered much in transmission. AP. give clue to the correct reading. 'I see this infatuation making you behave like a drunkard' (lit. methinks your drunkenness will make you roll on the road). *Soṇḍīra* (= *śauṇḍīra*) from *śauṇḍa*, excited, intoxicated, drunk.

P. 17. l. 9. m u d d h a m u h i (= *mugdhamukhi*),—*mugdha* here means 'lovely', 'charming.'

P. 18. l. 1. k h a l a k h a ṇ ḍ e h i ṃ. Skt. *khala* means 'earth'; hence the expression means 'by means of clods of earth'. Indian parents sometimes playfully provoke their small children by such expressions. With Karpūramañjarī this has been a modest way of disclosing her royal parentage. Cf. Lanman.

l. 16. e s ā ... d e h a n t a r e ṇ a. 'This earthly Sarasvatī is the goddess go-between incarnate'. 'The earthly Sarasvatī' is a humerous reference to the queen's appreciation of Vicakṣaṇā. With this remark the jester slyly hints that Vicakṣaṇā the queen's trusted maid will ultimately serve as the king's go-between for winning the love of Karpūramañjarī. The end of the story amply justifies such a view.

ACT. II.

P. 20, l. 9. k a h a ṃ ... p a n t i o. Though the sense of this passage is quite clear from the context yet its literal meaning is not so. It seems that the reference is here to a dull boy who does not improve his writing and for a long time keeps on writing on the same set of palm-leaves (tāḍī) with washable ink. The word *tāḍī* seems to exists in the Bengali compound *pāt-tāḍī* পাত্তাড়ি meaning probably '(plantain) leaves and palm (leaves)'.

l. 11. t a g g a a - h i d a ā v a j j a ṃ—the affliction of the heart in connection with her; *āvajjaṃ* (= **āpadyam*). Southern mss. read here *māṇasam* which is evidently an emendation for *āvajjam*.

l. 19. p ā l i t t i ā = **pālitrikā* = **pāritrikā* from the root *pār* to take across.

P. 21. l. 4. c i t t e v a h u ṭ ṭ a d i ṇ a h u ṭ ṭ a d i (*avaghṛṣṭati>vaghṛṣṭati*), lit. she rubs herself to my heart (P. reads *vahuṭṭadi* and W. *ca huṭṭadi,*) 'she does not fall short of or diminish (even after rubbing herself)'.

P. 22. l. 6. k a j j ā v a ā r a k ā l a (=*kāryâvatāra*°)— 'time for getting into business'.

P. 23. l. 6. H a r a b a l l a h ā e d e v ī e d e v ī a c c i d ā (=*Haraballabhāyai devyai devī arcitā*),— *arcitā* is here *akarmake kartari kta* (=*dā*). Konow's emendation is unneccessery.

P. 24. l. 4, d ī h a r ā—Is the origin of this word a hypothetical **dīghara* as opposed to *dīrgha* (Skt.). Bengali *dīghal* দীঘল is based on a Prakrit **digghala*.

l. 11. ṇ ī s ā s ā etc. Lanman's translation of this stanza is not altogether right ; *ṇīsāsā* ... *pasaraṇā* means 'sighs as long as the pearl-string,' *i.e.* very deep.

c a n d a ṇ u c c o ḍ a k ā r ī means 'drying up the sandal (applied on the breast for cooling the body).'

P. 25. l. 10. v a t t a ṃ is equivalent to either Skt. *vṛttaṃ* or *vārtāṃ*.

P. 26. l. 2, k h a r a p a v a ṇ a - p a ṇ o l l i a - d a l a g g ā. Konow reads *dara-* against *khara-* in the best ms. which is quite right here. By this adj. the princess wearing a green *sari* has been compared to a plaintain plant the outer leaves (*dalagga*) of which have been turned down by violent wind (*khara-pavaṇa*) ; *dalagga* (=*dalâgraḥ*) means *agradalaḥ* 'outer leaves', for in Pkt. members of a compound are often arbitrarily placed. See Gaṅgādharabhaṭṭa's comm. to Gāthāsaptaśati, I. 1.

l. 6. m a a ṇ a t o ṇ ī r a ṃ (=*madana-tūṇīram*) quiver of the God of Love. The appropriateness of the simile lies in the fact that Madana has five arrows in his quiver and there are five fingers in a hand.

l. 13. l a l ā ḍ a l o l a g g a s a ṅ g i ṇ ī. This Pkt. compound too violates the word order prescribed in Skt. grammars. In Skt. it will be *lola-lalāṭāgrasaṅginī.*

P. 27. l. 1. d e v a i d a ṃ etc. Konow with mss. other than WS. puts this speech in the mouth of the jester. But considering the partiality he has for ornaments it appears to be wrong. See Notes on II. 25 below.

l. 11. m a e s a v v ā l a ṅ k i d ā v a ṇ ṇ i d ā. The jester has nowhere before described Karpūramañjarī with all her ornaments ; it may be that he is referring to some such description which he gave of the princess during the interval between the Act I. and Act II. This reference is merely a dramatic device to give emphasis to what he was going to say. It is possibly due to a misunderstanding of this passage that the stanza beginning with *Jissā diṭṭhi etc.* (II. 23.) has in some late mss. been put into the mouth of the jester, though W. allots this to Vicakṣaṇā.

l. 13. ṇ i s a g g a c a ṅ g a s s a ...... b h ū s a ṇ e-h i. The jester here stoutly gives his own view as opposed to the king's in I. 31. and provokes the latter's reply in the next passage.

l. 20. t h o r ā ṇ a ṃ etc. The substance of this stanza is : Toilet does not effect any improvement to a lady's full round breasts, her wide eyes, lovely face and her body; or, in other words, it puts things in a disadvantage; for example, clothes will cover the charming breasts, collyrium will put a black mark around the eyes, the natural grace of the face will be covered by the powder and the beautiful formation of the body will be obscured by garments. Still these will please all. Now what is the reason of this ? The remarkable reason of this is that anything that is beautiful by nature (*ruḍhie*) cannot be spoilt.

P. 28. l. 2. s u t t a v v a ṃ (=*śrotavyam*) lit. 'that which ought to be heard'; as an adj. to *kāraṇaṃ*, it means 'remarkable'; *kattavvaṃ* has influenced the formation of this word.

P. 28. l. 4. n a ḍ ī ṇ a ṃ v i ḍ a m b o. 'an imitation or deception of the actresses'. For the make-up of a *naṭī* see the Saṅgītaratnākara, VII, 1250-1257.

l. 5. ṇ i s a g g a ṃ.—'natural condition'. Konow reads 'niaṅgaṃ' against. W. ; *ṇisaggaṃ* gives a better sense to the passage.

l. 6. a d a ṃ b h o, honest, undeceitful ; *alambho* (for *alabbha*=*alabhya*) 'unattainable'.

l. 7. p a r a m a s u h a a r e k ā l e—'in that pleasant age' i. e., youth. Lanman's interpretation of the whole stanza is not in keeping with the spirit of the preceding passages.

P. 29. l. 4. p ā i ā j u ṇ ṇ a - m a j j ā r i ā ... t a k k a ṃ. Here Konow unnecessarily disregards the testimony of W. The expression means 'The old cat has been made to drink the buttermilk as milk'. W. puts this passage in the mouth of the king. This seems to be only right. The king was only *thinking* in these terms and in our modern taste it is bad enough. An *open reference* to the queen as an old cat would have been a piece of impudence on the part of the jester to whom the later mss. ascribe it. Considering the caution the jester displays later on (II. 47³.) Konow's ascription of the speech to him seems to be quite unjustified.

l. 19. u c c e h i ṃ g o ü r e h i ṃ etc. This passage seems to have been much damaged in transmission. An ignorance of the exact construction of the swing might possibly have been responsible for this. For aught we know the swing on which Karpūramañjarī was placed was something like the body of an Indian chariot and as such it had steeples (*gopura*) and banners (*dhvaja*) and bells (*ghaṇṭā*), due to all of which it had the similarity of a heavenly car carrying a goddess. The sort of swing that is used in the swing-festival of Kṛṣṇa should be remembered in this connexion.

P. 30. l. 11. u v a r i ṭ ṭ h i a t h a ṇ a p p a b b h ā r a-c a m p i a ṃ etc. In W. alternative lines of this and the seven succeeding stanzas have been divided between the jester and the king. The king praises the heroine with short descriptions (*sutta* = *sūtra*) of her charm and the jester makes comments (*vitti* = *vṛtti*) on the same. See l. 8 above. But Konow overlooked this fact. *campia* : This is a deśī word which means 'pressing'. It is probably connected with the Bengali root *cāpā* চাপা to press.

l. 19. t ā r a ṃ—'clearly', 'excellently'. In this stanza the gracefully moving white pearl string has been compared to a stream which sprinkles the creeper of Cupid's exploits with water.

P. 31. l. 4. g h u s i ṇ a (= **ghṛṣṇa* = *ghṛṣṭa*) 'rubbed'.

l. 10. s i l i m m u h e. Two arrows being two eyes. Here too Rāj. has used dual, an unusual thing for Pkt. Grammarians however will consider this to be plural.

P. 32. l. 8. a ī s i s i r a ṃ - p i etc. *Himānī* means here the cold season. The whole expression means, 'though the winter is very cold, yet it seems to be as hot as the the summer midday'.

l. 10. l a c c h ī s a h a a r o.—'alone' (lit. *lakṣmī* or *Rājalakṣmī* as his companion) ; cf. *kṛpāṇamātradvitīya*

......*samāyāto' si*, Jambhaladatta's Version of the Vetāla-pañca-viṃśati, ed. M. B. Emeneau, p. 10, lines 11-12.

l. 13. s a ṇ ṇ i h i d o...... m a n t ī h i ṃ. *mantīhiṃ* in this passage has been read by Konow as *sahihiṃ* against W. and other mss. But this seems to be unnecessary. King's friends were also a kind of *mantrin* or *saciva* (ninister) to him ; cf. *iyaṃ imassa kāmatantasaïvassa ṇīdī*, Mālavikāgnimitra, IV. 181 (ed. Pandit)

P. 33. l. 17. k ī s a t ī e d u v ā r a d e s e b h a v i-d a v v a ṃ—'Why should she (Karpūramañjarī) stop at the door ?' Lanman's translation seems to be wrong ; for Vicakṣaṇā already (ll. 14, 15 above) tells the jester that they should stay there for the mutual meeting of the king and Karpūramañjarī. On this the jester enquires of Vicakṣaṇā what reasons will bring Karpūramañjarī at the door of the Emerald Bower.

P. 35. l. 4. j a t t ā (=*yātrā*) ' rush', lit. 'start'.

s a m a t t ā (=*samāptā*) 'entire'.

l. 12. k a j j a l a k a l ā s a ṃ v a g g i d ā ṇ a ṃ' 'made prominent (*saṃvaggida*=*saṃvargita*) by the art of (giving) collyrium.' Konow's reading is opposed to W. and does not carry any good sense.

P. 36. l. 1. s i h ā s u (=*śikhāsu*) 'in branches',

l. 10 t ī e 'by her', i. e. by the Śrī or the goddess of beauty referred to in previous half of the couplet.

l. 12. b ā l ā o. Konow reads *bālāu*, but it should be emended even against W.

ACT. III.

P. 38. l. 4 o l l o l l ā i-v i—(=ārdrārdrā-pi) 'even very liquid', molten gold has a very bright yellow colour.

l. 8. t ā r ā (=tārāḥ), 'excellent'.

l. 10, r a h a s a-v a l i a k a ṇ ṭ h ī 'one who forcibly makes (others) turn (their) head (lit. neck)'. Lanman's interpretation can hardly be supported.

l. 11. s a v a ṇ a p a h a ṇ i v i ṭṭ h a 'entering the region of ears', i. e. very large. Lanman's translation does not seem to be accurate.

l. 18. h a t t h a n t a r e 'one cubit apart'.

P. 41. l. 5. ṇ a h a b a h a l i d a j o h ṇ ā ṇ i b b h a r e etc. In the night that was filled with the moonlight that made the sky ample. Here also we find Pkt. word-order in the first part of the compound. According to Skt. grammar the compound would be *bahalidaṇaha-johṇā.* Konow's reading seems to impoverish the sense.

l. 10. s u v i ṇ a a ... a b h i p p ā o. The first half of the passage has been much distorted in all mss. except PWNOR. From *suviṇaa* we have Old Beng. *suiṇā* সুইণা.

a ṇ u s a n d h a m ā ṇ a 'here means 'comforting', cf. *ātmānam anusandhehi.* Hitopadeśa 4. 3. (ref. of Apte's Skt. Dictionary).

P. 42. l. 19. c i t t a b h e o (=*citra-bhedaḥ*), 'a peculiar distinction' (from the previous condition).

P. 45. l. 10. k a r a ṇ i g g a d a ṃ 'coming out from the hands' ; but such an expression does not well fit in with the context. The original reading was perhaps *karaṇilaggaṃ* 'coming in close contact with the hands', but this is not given in any of the mss.

l. 16. g a ṇ ṭ h i v a ṇ ṇ a...h a r i ṇ e h i. See notes on Vikramorvaśī 1. 17 (ref. of Apte's Skt. Dictionary) *luḍijjanti=loḍyante.*

P. 46. l. 12. m a j j h a a ṃ (=madhyakam) lit. 'the slender middle portion' i. e. waist. cf. Bengali *mājā* মাজা.

P. 47. l. 3. k a h a ṃ v a r i l l a ñ c a l e ṇ a etc. This puting out of the lamp by the jester was occasioned by Rāj. with a view to give the king an opportunity to make advances to Karpūramañjarī who was a *bālā* (maiden) and hence was naturally shy. See Vātsyāyana (II. 2. 10) *bālāyā apūrvāyāś cāndhakāre* 'a girl who was not approached before (by any other man) should be approached in darkness'.

l. 11. ṇ a v a s s a t a ü s a s s a (*navasya trapusasya*) 'of a young cucumber (which has thorns sharp and prickly)' ; horripilation at the touch of a person of the opposite sex has been considered as making the body thorny, standing hairs being compared with these thorns. This word has wrongly been displaced by *timisa* omission of which by Roxburgh was only natural. cf. Lanman's note on *timisa.*

P. 48. l. 19. s a s i h a r a-r a ī a m a r a ṭ ṭ o The pride of the moon (*sasihara=saśadhara*) and the sun (*raī=ravi*). The stanza refers to late Indian spring which is another name for summer characterized by the hot sun and the pleasant moon (see Ṛtusaṃhāra I.1).

P. 50. l. 1. d e v ī e p i a v a a s s e ṇ a etc. This speech has been preceded in Konow's ed. by the exit and re-entrance of Kuraṅgikā. But this is unnecessary. Before her going the jester infers the real reason of the noise. This passage means : 'the deception practised by the dear friend (king) on the queen being found out, she comes...' The Skt. translation will make it clear ; devyai priyavayasyasya vañcanākṛtaṃ avagamya (sā) āgacchati.

l. 2. t ā k u j j a v ā m a ṇ a - etc.—Though Konow puts this in the mouth of Kuraṅgikā it should be the continuation of what the jester was saying. Mss. PNT support such a view.

ACT. IV.

P. 51. l. 2. a h o g ā ḍ h a a r o a m h a g i m h o. In stead of this sentence and two succeeding ones Konow reads a couplet, but W. reads prose. So do PNOR. But the second part of the couplet does not at all occur in them.

l. 5. s u h a a j a ṇ a.—'a beautiful person.'

l. 7. v a h a ṇ i j j a (= **vadhanīya* = *vadhya*) 'liable to be struck or to be killed'; the *root* 'han' means 'to strike or to kill.' Konow's *vādhaṇijja* (= **vādhanīya*) means 'liable to put obstacle or trouble.'

l. 9. k i ṃ ṇ u k h u d e 'etc.—This passage and the five succeeding ones do not seem to have any organic connexion with the plot of the play. It is possible that a portion of it containing relevant passages have been lost or this portion has accidentally crept in.

P. 52. l. 2. t a l i ṇ a v i t t h a r ā 'of short duration.'

l. 7. m a j j h a ṇ h e s i r i k h a ṇ ḍ a - etc. In this stanza Rāj. suggests a new set of five objects as Love's arrows.

P. 53. l. 4. l ī l u t t a ṃ s e s i r ī s a ṃ etc. Lanman's translation of this stanza is defective. *liluttaṃse sirīsaṃ* means '*Sirīṣa* flower at the sporting crest'; *sindhuvāra* here means S. flower and not S. berry as Lanman takes it. Konow's reading of the stanza is also not defensible. In the third foot should be read *kāmavijjo* (^{0}*vidyaḥ*); *maṇojja* meaning 'endowed with love-charm, and pleasing'.

l. 14. p a c c a g g a ṃ ṇ a v a r ū v a etc. This quarter of the stanza has been badly changed in mss. other than WOR, because of its difficulty. W too does not seem to give it aright.

P. 54. l. 5. a ṇ a ṅ g a s e n ā - k a l i ṅ g a s e ṇ ā etc. The speech of the jester containing the names of many maid-servants has been much distorted in later times.

l. 16. ā ḍ h a t t ā o (= *ādhṛtāḥ*) 'assigned', 'placed'.

P. 55. l. 11. t a l i ṇ a ṃ s u ā o 'having thin clothes'. Skt. *talina* means 'thin'. Lanman's translation here seems to be wrong The use of this adj. to clothes suggests that they being drenched the voluptuous charm of the dancer's physical form became visible.

l. 12. j a n t a j a l e ṇ a ṃ m a ṇ i b h ā i ṇ e h ī ṃ with water from syringe as well as jewelled cups. Of the meaning of *maṇibhāiṇa* we are not sure.

l. 14. s o l a h a—(= *ṣoḍaśa* ⊳ *soḍasa* ⊳ *solasa* ⊳ *solaha*.) This word gives Beng. *ṣola* (= *śola*) ষোল.

n a c c a ṇ ī. It is cognate with Beng. *nācanī*, *nācunī* নাচনী, নাচুনী 'dancer'.

l. 16. r e h ā - v i s u d d h ā. Observing correct *rehā* (= *rekhā*). For the meaning of *rekhā*. see the Abhinayadarpaṇa, p. 27.

l. 18. m o t t ū ṇ a...v ā r a ā ī 'leaving aside jewelled cups'. See *maṇivāraehiṃ* above.

P. 56. l. 1. t i k a ṇ ḍ a c ā v ā (= *tṛkāṇḍacāpāḥ*) 'having three arrows and a bow'.

l. 2. p u l i n d a. An aboriginal tribe dwelling in jungles.

l. 5. h u ḍ u k k ā (= *ḍamaru*). See the Saṅgītaratnākara, VI ; 1072.

l. 8. j o i ṇ ī v a l a a. Konow seems to be wrong in separating this into three parts. It means the bracelets of a Yoginī who wore iron bangles. The passage appears to be corrupt.

P. 57. l. 11. s ī s e s a p p o etc. Cf. Mudrārākṣasa, I. 22.

l. 16. a g g a d o d a k k h i ṇ ā v i h i d o .... v i v ā h a b h a v i s s a d i. It seems that this passage, occuring in NO has been considered difficult and unmeaning and hence discarded. It means 'next (*agrataḥ*) the marriage which is demanded as *dakṣiṇā* will take place.'

P. 58. l. 2. p a j j a r ā v e d i. (=**prakṣarāpayati*) W. reads here wrongly *pabbhavedi.*

ṇ a h u s a r a a s a m ī r a m a n t a r e ṇ a...... This passage though occurring in W.* between *-vedi* and *sehāliā-* has been given up in some mss. and by Konow. But this has spoilt the passage. Cf. Viddhaśāla., p. 634.

P. 60 l. 1. p a r i s a r e a p p a ṇ o 'in one's own proximity', 'neighbourhood'. Konow reads here *pari-sappiṇā* with PN.

l. 9. j a n ā n t i k a ṃ. No ms. gives this, but from the context this is to be assumed.

l. 10. p ā r i d d h i ā (=*pāridhvajikā*), -ddhaïā ⊳ -ddhia. This word means 'standard-bearer'.

l. 12. s u t t i ā (*sūtrikā*) 'string'.

P. 61. l. 3. p a ḍ i v a ṇ ṇ a ṃ (=*prativarṇaṃ*) 'dress', 'costume'.

m u d d h ā (*mugdhā*) 'very young'.

T h e E n d.

ADDITIONS AND CORRECTIONS

P. XXII. line 3 *read* 'possible not' *for* 'not possible'.

P. XXVIII: last line but one. *Read* syāma ity adhyeyaṃ Vyākaraṇam.

P. XXXII. line 2. *For* 'we shall discuss it later' *read* 'it appears that the doubling might be merely a graphic device to indicate that the vowel following the double consonant, was accented and this accent left no room for the elision of the non-aspirate stop concerned.

P. XLI. line 10. *Add.* See Notes on P. 5 line 6.

P. XLVII. Between paragraphs 20 and 21 *Read* :

II. KARPURAMANJARI

P. LXIX. last line. *For* '*pratiloma*' *read* '*anuloma*'.

P. 1 line 12 *Read* ०सिप्पीम.

P. 2 „ 6 *For* सज्जोज्जन्ति *read* सज्जिज्जन्ति.

P. 6 „ 6 „ ०वम्भवं *read* ०बम्भवं.

P. 7 „ 7 „ तड्डिसंघड्डिदे *read* तुट्टसंघडिदे.

P. 8 „ 3 *Read* ०कद्दत्तणेण.

„ 8 „ खलिदा.

P. 10 „ 14 *For* असोअतक *read* असोअतरू.

„ 1 *Read* हरिउड्ढ०

P. 12 „ 3 *Put one* '।' (*daṇḍa* = fullstop) *after* बम्भणो.

P. 13 „ 18 for दट्ठूं *read* दट्ठुं.

20 *Add to the foot-note* 1 :
See the Prākṛtapaiṅgala p. 428.

21 *Add to the foot-note* 4 : See the entire stanza quoted in the comm. of Dhanika on *Daśarūpa* III. 15.

P. 15 „ 12 *Read* सुणिज्जदि.

„ 18 *for* जोह्णाए *read* जोण्हाए.

P. 16 „ 3 *read* वेढिदुं.

„ 15 „ सोण्डीरत्तणं.

„ 19 *for* ०मुणइ *read* ०मुद्ठिइ.

P. 20 „ 14 *Read* देव्वा दीहं मइ०

„ 18 „ अत्थाणीजण०

P. 21 „ 5 „ विसइदि.

„ 12 „ तिलजलञ्जलि०

P. 16 „ 16 „ दुक्खाणं

P. 24 Numbers 12 and 16 in the margin have been wrongly put against 13th and 17th lines respectively.

P. 25 line 1 *Read* पिअवअस्सस्स

P. 25 lines 11-12 *Read* कदं *for* किदं *and for see* v. l. *see* Konow's ed., *and see also* p. LIII. lines 15ff.

P. 27 line 14 *Read* मणीणं जडाणं

„ 21 „ सुद्धस्स *after* भूअन्दस्स

P. 29 „ 11 „ इत्तम् उदास.

P. 30 „ „ एन्ती जन्ती-च.

„ झणझणन्त^0.

P. 32 „ 3 „ वालिन्दु.

„ 4 „ वणाणं.

„ 5 „ अज्जलक्खुट्ठअदि.

„ 15 „ अच्छरिअं.

P. 33 „ 15 „ सिसिरोवआर०

P. 35 „ 14 „ मअच्छीए.

P. 36 „ 2 „ ठिदं च गअणं

„ 4 „ कारणं

„ 12 „ वालाओ.

„ 18 „ माणिणी०

P. 38 „ 18 „ कन्दोट्ट च

P. 44 „ 10 „ दुवे
P. 45 „ 12 „ सुदं
P. 47 „ 14 „ [6]सुहाणुबन्धणो
„ 15 „ भूमी०
P. 48 „ 16 „ [4]सरपजल[0].
P. 49 „ 8 „ चोहिइत्ति for चोहि इत्ति
P. 56 „ 9 „ कोदुहल्ल१सजक्कम०
P. 64 „ 29 „ s a m m o h a ṇ ā s ā ṇ a.
P. 65 „ last but one *Read* ṭ h a v i d o *for* ṭhāvido.
P. 66 „ 9 *read* '*muaṅga* (=*mṛdaṅga*)'.
P. 67 „ 17 „ ṛ > u seems to be no exclusive.
P. 68 „ 7 from the bottom. *Omit* jhā झा.
P. 69 „ last but one, *Read* : See p. 71 last line.
P. 71 „ 5 from the bottom. *Read* this from.
„ last. *After* 'best one' *add* :

Mārkaṇḍeya thinks that *peccha* is a substitute of *paśya* while *pekkha* comes from *prekṣa*. See Prākṛta-sarvasva, ed. Bhaṭṭanātha Svāmī, ix. 112.

P. 72 line 11 from the bottom '*Read potthāi*'.
8 „ „ *Read* : *potthāi for potthiāi* and *pustādi* for *pustakādi*

P. 88 line 6 from the bottom. *Omit the semicolon before* '*maṇojja*'.

P. 77 line 19 *After the fullstop, read* :

line 12. p a s ā h a ṇ ā-l a c c h ī. The first member of this compound word has here retained its gender. This is a peculiarity of Pkt.

P. 81 lines 7, 8 *Read* 'H a r a v a l l a h ā e' *and* 'Haravallabhāyai'.